Peak District

Ian Johnson

This book is dedicated to the memory of
Geoff Leeson 1931 - 2011

His warmth and humour
are ours forever

Peak District walks for all the family

central area

21 walks from 1 3/4 to 4 3/4 miles
Large scale maps
Illustrated throughout
Items of interest en route
Grid references for GPS waypoints

Ian Johnson
Johnson Publishing

Published by;
Johnson Publishing
160 Sutton Road
Mansfield
Notts NG18 5HH
email: johnson.publishing@virgin.net
website: www.peakdistrictbooks.co.uk

Published 2012

All route maps are based on 1940s Ordnance Survey Provisional Edition 1:25000 maps and revised from field surveys made by Johnson Publishing in 2011. The maps on pages 14 and 15 are based on Bartholomew's map of the Peak District 1935, updated by Johnson Publishing in 2011. Every effort has been made to ensure that the information given in this book is accurate. The publisher accepts no responsibility for any loss, injury or inconvenience caused to anyone whilst using this book.

ISBN 978-0-95425-748-4

Printed by Linney Group, Mansfield, Nottinghamshire

Contents

Acknowledgements

This book wouldn't have been possible without the help and encouragement of the following people. My mother Margaret Johnson, Anne Brimer, Alan Woods, Trevor Lowe and Sandy for accompanying me on most of the walks and for making useful suggestions.

All the walk directions have been thoroughly checked by experienced walkers Rod Dean and John Price. They have walked each one and pointed out errors and made suggestions for improvement. All the routes have been walked twice and some have been walked three or four times. Thanks are also due to Rod Dean for providing most of the natural history information and to John Price for checking and providing some of the grid reference data.

I have also been assisted from time to time by the staff at the Peak District National Park Authority.

I am grateful to The Dowager Duchess of Devonshire for allowing me to use information from her informative and entertaining book 'Round About Chatsworth,' Published by Frances Lincoln, 2005.

Thanks also to www.peakdistrictonline.co.uk for permission to use information on Bretton Clough, contained on pages 97 and 99.

Thanks to John Price and Rod Dean for proof reading. However any errors remaining within the book of any kind, are the responsibility of the author.

Introduction

The area chosen for the walks in this book is more or less what I have called the 'central area' of the Peak District National Park. There are also four walks outside the park boundary around Crich, Matlock and Matlock Bath. The Peak District has a great variety of landscapes from moorlands, and rocky edges to spectacular limestone dales and rich grassland. These two contrasting types of landscape are often referred to as the Dark Peak and White Peak. The underlying rock of the Dark Peak is gritstone, whilst the White Peak is limestone. The former is largely to the northern and eastern edges of the Peak District, whilst the latter forms the central and southern areas.

This guidebook includes both types of landscape, from the rocky gritstone of Froggatt Edge to the beautiful limestone dales such as Lathkill Dale and Cressbrook Dale. The area covered in this book is quite compact. The most northerly walk is at Eyam, with Crich being at the southern boundary, a distance of only about 16 miles. This means that you shouldn't have to waste a lot of time travelling between walks.

The Walks

We hope that the walks will be enjoyed by everyone. Whilst the book has been planned mainly for families with younger children, we hope that it will be used by people of all ages. For each route we have included information likely to be of interest, such as industrial history, geology, natural history and anything else relevant to the area. We have tried to plan the routes so that long, steep or rocky sections are avoided. This hasn't always been possible of course, but they have been kept to a minimum.

Walking safely

Road walking and crossings of busy roads have been kept to a minimum. Take extra care when walking along lanes and at road crossings. Some of the walks are along the rocky gritstone edges and one walk ascends High Tor, Matlock Bath. On these walks the paths run parallel to unprotected sheer edges. It is important to keep children and dogs under close control and ensure they stay a safe distance away from any edges. In any case dogs should be on a lead when walking through areas with livestock.

Equipment

I advise walkers to wear comfortable walking boots or trail shoes. Some of the routes can become very muddy after rain. Even at the relatively low altitudes of the walks in this book the weather can change suddenly for the worse. Take waterproofs and additional layers of clothing. Some food and liquid should also be carried. Whilst the mapping in the guide is as accurate as possible, I would recommend taking the OS 1:25,000 scale White Peak, Explorer OL24 map and a compass.

Starting Points

All the walks begin from a convenient parking area, either a car park, roadside parking or a lay-by. On pages 18 to 21, there are detailed road maps and instructions to help you find the parking areas. I have given grid references to help locate the points, abbreviated to GR in the text. Where a walk starts from roadside parking, it doesn't interfere with residents' parking. Several of the walks start from car parks run by the Peak District National Park Authority. For an annual permit ring 01629 816211 or email: parking.permits@peakdistrict.gov.uk.

Public Transport

Many of the walks are accessible by bus. There is a 'Peak District Bus Timetable,' available from tourist information centres, libraries and newsagents. Public transport information is also available at www.peakdistrict.gov.uk and www.derbyshire.gov.uk.

Heights

The maximum height attained on each walk is given on the map page and obtained from the OS map. The figure for the total ascent is intended for reference only and as a comparison between walks. It may be subject to error.

Distances

The distances given for the walks have been obtained by using a hand-held GPS navigation unit. They are given in miles, with kilometres in brackets. Distances have been rounded up or down to the nearest 1/4 mile.

Walking Times

The times given for each walk are for guidance only. They allow time for short breaks etc. As a guide, I consider that 2 miles per hour average walking speed, is about right when walking with younger children. Of course everyone has their own idea of what is a comfortable walking speed and you may have to adjust the times accordingly.

Photo locations

The green arrow and number beneath most of the photos correspond with those on the small map. They indicate the approximate position and angle that the photo was taken.

Rights of Way

Most of the routes use public footpaths and public bridleways. Some routes use concessionary paths, this is where the landowner allows the public to use a route, without it being legally designated as a right of way. One such route in this book is the section following the River Wye, between the former Cressbrook and Litton mills. Some paths don't fall into any of the above types, they are paths or tracks that are in free and general use.

Most path signage uses the standard colour-coded arrows; yellow for public footpaths, blue for public bridleways and white for concessionary paths.

Three walks in this guide use sections of the Monsal Trail, which runs along a disused rail line. It was part of the Midland Line between London and Manchester, built in 1867 and closed in 1968. Now that the previously closed tunnels have been re-opened in 2011, it is possible to walk and cycle the whole route without having to do any diversions.

Introduction

The Route Directions

All the directions in this book have been compiled with great care. They have been double-checked by people who have many years' experience of walking in the Peak District. However if any errors remain, they are entirely my responsibility.

The numbers on the map cross-reference with the corresponding numbered instructions on the page opposite. This helps you to keep track of where you are on the map at each of the numbered instructions. As an additional check, a grid reference is given for each of the map numbers. These can be keyed in to a GPS device and used as waypoints as an optional aid in following the route. The figures in the column 'miles' next to the grid references column gives the cumulative mileage at each point. Walk directions always appear on the facing page to a map, to save having to flick pages between the map and directions.

Items of interest along the route

For clarity and ease of use, the text printed in green is extra information relating to things seen on the walk. The black text gives instructions.

Mountain Rescue

Mountain rescue is co-ordinated by the police. If you need assistance dial 999. Be aware that you cannot rely on mobile phone reception in some areas of the Peak District.

The Maps

Each walk has a route map facing the walk directions page. See the key to symbols used on page 16. All maps have north pointing to the top of the page. The scale of each map is shown along the bottom edge. The heights are shown in feet and the contour lines indicate 25 feet intervals. Whilst it is not essential to carry an Ordnance Survey map with you on the walks, we recommend you take one. It will be invaluable if you go wrong (hopefully unlikely) and it may add to your enjoyment of the walk. All the walks fall within the OS. OL24 Explorer, White Peak 1:25000.

Grid references and GPS devices

Don't worry, you do not need to understand grid references or use a GPS unit in order to use this book. The walks can be done perfectly well using the instructions and the route maps alone. However if you do have a hand-held GPS device you may wish to key in the provided grid references for a route and use these as waypoints during the walk, as an aid to navigation. Even if you don't intend using the grid references or a GPS for these walks, you may find the following information useful in the future.

Under the British National Grid system the country is divided up into four squares of 500 by 500 km. Each of the squares is lettered - S, T, N, and H. This gives us the first letter of a grid reference. These four squares are each subdivided into 25 squares of 100 by 100 km. Each square is lettered, starting with A at the top left corner and Z at the bottom right corner. This forms the second letter of a grid reference.

Maps are divided into kilometre squares. If you look along the bottom and top margins of any Ordnance Survey map (or any other mapping, using the British National Grid system) you will see that the vertical lines are each numbered with two digits. Likewise the horizontal lines are numbered with two digits along the left and right margins of the map. Dividing the map up into squares enables us to give coordinates that locate within which square lies a particular point or feature.

A grid reference is always two letters followed by an equal number of digits that tells us how far east and how far north a particular square lies within the grid. Therefore the readings taken from the map are termed eastings and northings. Eastings are always given first and northings second. The numbers at the end of the vertical lines at the top and bottom margins of a map are the eastings. The numbers at the ends of the horizontal lines, at the left and right margins of the map are northings. Another way to remember which are the eastings and which the northings is this. The numbers that increase as you go east across the map are eastings and the numbers that increase as you go north up the map are northings. In the example below we need to specify a grid reference for the summit of Fin Cop (the red dot). From Fin Cop look at the black grid line to the west and read the two numbers at the end of the line, on the south margin. In this case it is 17. This is the Easting. Then take the black grid line to the south of the point and read off the numbers at the end of the line on the west margin. This is the Northing. In this case it is 70. So the four digit grid reference for Fin Cop summit would be 1770. This isn't accurate enough for navigation as it only tells us the feature lies within a 1 km square.

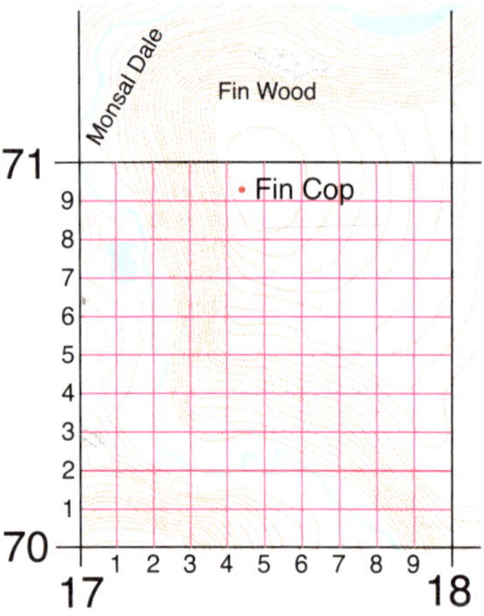

To give a grid reference locating the point within a 1/10th square km, we divide it by ten along each axis. In our example I have added the pink lines to indicate the km square being divided up into 100 squares of 100m x 100m. Of course on the OS map you will either have to estimate, or use a romer. This is a piece of clear plastic overprinted with squares matching a km square on 1:25,000 and 1:50,000 scale maps. This is overlaid on the map, aligned with the appropriate km square. An overprinted grid divides the square as shown above. We can now give a six digit grid reference. You obtain the third digit for the easting and the northing in the same way as the first two numbers were obtained - i.e. take the line to the west of Fin Cop, read the number at the bottom of the line (on the romer). In this case it is 4. This is the third digit of the Easting and indicates the point lies in a square 4/10ths east along the km square. Then take the line to the south of Fin Cop and read the number at the end of the line. It is 9. This is the third digit of the Northing. So the point lies within a square 100m x 100m, 4/10ths east and 9/10ths north within the km square represented by the four digit grid reference 1770. The resulting six digit grid reference is 174709. With practice you can estimate the 1/10ths without using a romer.

Using the same method, an eight digit grid reference would locate a point within an area of only 10m x 10m square. With a romer you can obtain an eight digit reading, using the same method - in this case the fourth easting digit would be 4, and the fourth northing digit would be 3. So the eight digit grid reference for Fin Cop summit would be 17447093. You now need the two letters which represent the area covered by the part of the map that you are using - in this case it is SK. (The White Peak OS map is mainly in the area denoted by SK, with the western section being SJ). The appropriate two letters precede the digits to form the full grid reference, giving SK17447093. An eight digit grid reference enables features to be located with accuracy.

A ten digit grid reference, would locate a point to within a 1 metre square. Taking a ten digit reading from a map though isn't possible, as the area on the map is too small.

Most hand-held GPS devices however give a ten digit grid reference. That is why I have used ten digits within the book. In practice however the accuracy of a GPS unit will vary depending on a number of external factors. In general use, if you wish to input a grid reference to a GPS unit to use as a waypoint you need to key in the appropriate two letters followed by ten digits. You can obtain eight digit grid references from the map and just add a zero for the fifth digit of the easting and the northing. Of course you can also add routes and waypoints digitally.

Changes over time

During the life of this book some of the instructions may be rendered incorrect by changes to gates or stiles, the removal or addition of walls and fences, house building etc.

The Peak District National Park and surrounding area

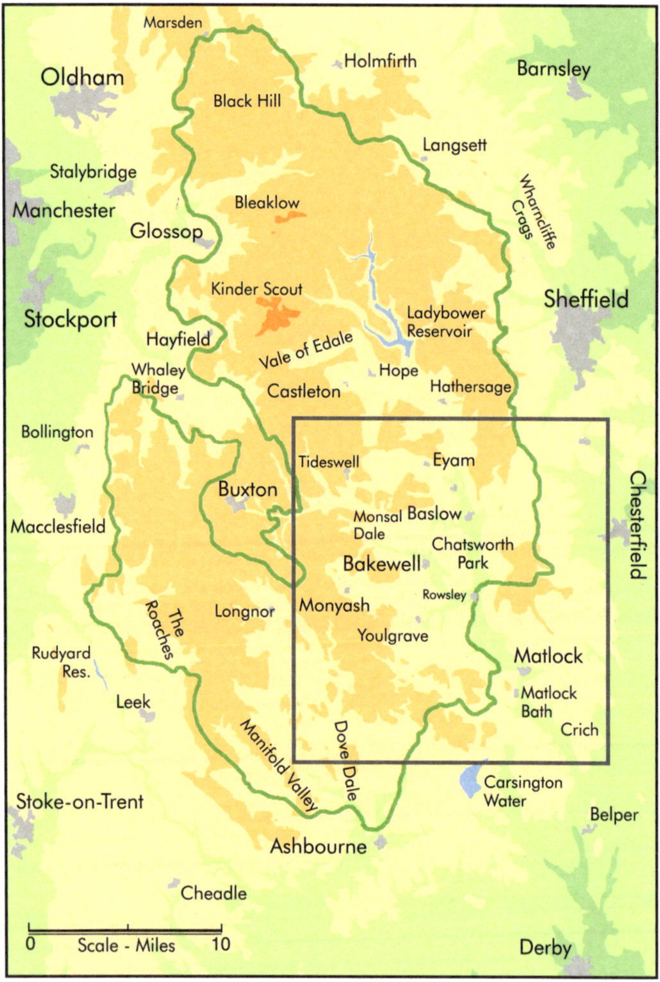

National Park boundary

Enlargement of inset on map opposite

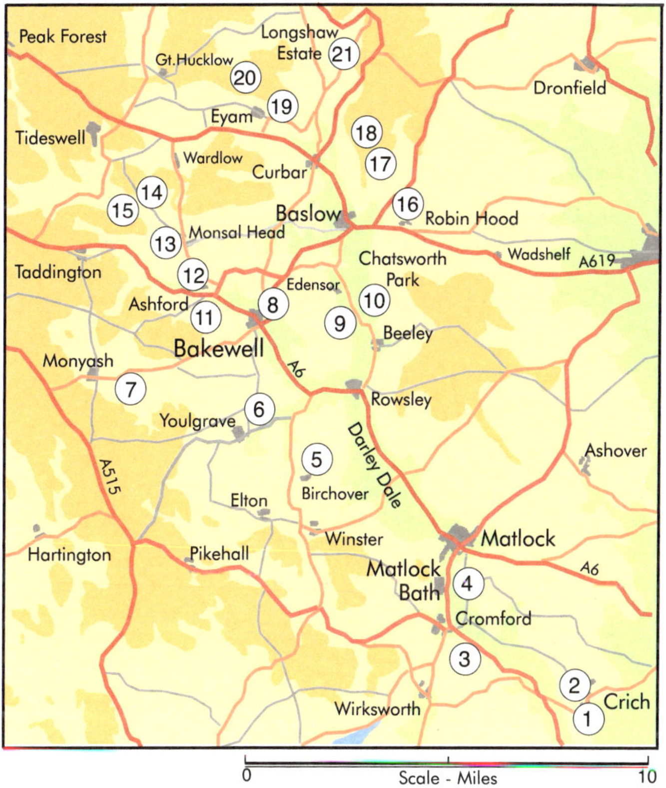

Key to map above and on opposite page -

Heights -

- Sea level to 250 feet
- 250 to 500 feet
- 500 to 1000 feet
- 1000 to 2000 feet
- Above 2000 feet

(1) Approximate location of walk

- Roads classified as 'A' roads
- Roads classified as 'B' roads
- Unclassified roads

Key to the walking route maps

	Walking route; tunnel section
	Suggested detour or alternative route
	Walking route - road sections
	Other paths, not on the route
	Main roads
	Minor roads
P	Designated parking area
②	Location of corresponding route instruction
	Indicated direction in which to walk
N	Direction of north on the map
	Field boundary
200	Contour lines (25 feet intervals)
	Buildings and built-up areas
	Rocks and rock features
	Lake or pond
	River or stream
1124 △	Triangulation Pillar - height shown in feet. (White concrete pillars - abbreviated to 'trig. point').
	Place of worship
1	Location and angle of view of photograph.
PH	Public House

Walks List

Starting Point locator map for Walks 1 - 10

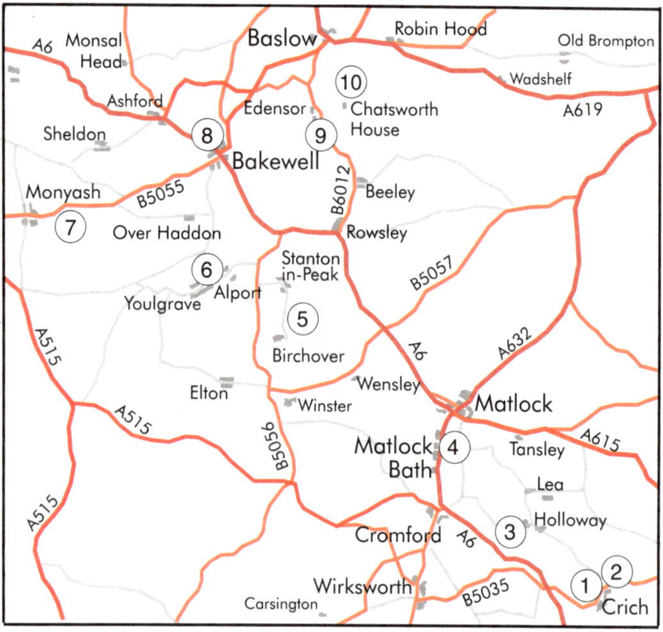

Directions to parking locations and relevant information

Walk	Title (abbreviated)	Starting Point	Grid Reference	Page
1	Crich Chase	Crich	SK34855420	22
2	Crich Memorial	Crich	SK34855420	26

Directions: From the A6, from the Matlock direction, turn left after the bridge at Whatstandwell, onto the B5035. In Crich, the Market Place parking area is on the left. Free parking. If there is no space available may be roadside parking near the Black Swan on the right-hand side.

Walk	Title	Starting Point	Grid Reference	Page
3	High Peak Junction	H.P.J. car park	SK31544610	30

Directions: From the A6 travelling from the south. At Cromford, turn right at the traffic lights. Go past Arkwright's Mill, over the River Derwent and in 1 1/4 miles turn right into the High Peak Junction car park.

Walk	Title	Starting Point	Grid Reference	Page
4	High Tor	Artist Corner	SK29715955	34

Directions to parking locations and relevant information

Directions: The Artist Corner pay-and-display car park is on the A6 between Matlock and Matlock Bath. It is about $\frac{1}{2}$ mile south from the centre of Matlock - on the left if travelling from Matlock.

Walk	Title	Starting point	Grid Reference	Page
5	Stanton Moor	Roadside lay-bys	SK24196280	38

Directions: From the A6, Matlock direction. $1\frac{1}{4}$ miles past Rowsley turn left onto the B5056 signed 'Youlgrave.' In just under a mile, turn left (still the B5056) signed 'Ashbourne.' In $\frac{1}{3}$ mile ignore the first left to 'Stanton-in-Peak.' In another mile turn left signed 'Birchover.' Go up the hill, at the end of the village turn left, signed 'P.' Go past the Birchover Stone Quarry car park (free public parking in the lower part). The best lay-by is about 300 yards beyond on the right-hand side of the road. Another lay-by is on the left in about 100 yards. If these are full return to the quarry car park.

Walk	Title	Starting Point	Grid Reference	Page
6	Lathkill Dale (east)	Lay-bys, Alport	SK27966456	42

Directions: From the A6, from the Matlock direction. Keep on the A6 through Rowsley. In $1\frac{1}{4}$ miles turn left onto the B5056 signed 'Youlgrave.' In just under a mile ignore a left turn. Keep straight on. Alport is reached in about $\frac{1}{2}$ mile. Lay-bys on both sides of the road.

Walk	Title	Starting Point	Grid Reference	Page
7	Lathkill Dale (west)	Lay-by, nr. Monyash	SK1572665	46

Directions: From the A515 Buxton to Ashbourne road. Take the B5055, signed 'Monyash, Bakewell.' Go through the village and in $\frac{1}{2}$ mile there is a lay-by on the left-hand side and parking at the toilets opposite.

Walk	Title	Starting Point	Grid Reference	Page
8	Bakewell	Agricultural Centre	SK22096874	50

Directions: The Agricultural Centre car park is about $\frac{1}{2}$ mile from Bakewell town centre off the A6, Bakewell to Matlock road. It is signed to the left as 'town centre car park.' Pay-and-display. **Closed Mondays.**

Walk	Title	Starting Point	Grid Reference	Page
9	Edensor	Calton Lees car pk.	SK25876849	54

Directions: Off the B6012. About $\frac{3}{4}$ mile past Chatsworth House (from the Baslow direction). Or from the A6. Leave at Rowsley, turn onto the B6012. The car park is signed to the left after $1\frac{1}{2}$ miles. Fee payable.

Walk	Title	Starting Point	Grid Reference	Page
10	Hunting Tower	Chatsworth House	SK26197034	58

Directions: From the B6012. Follow signs for Chatsworth House car park. Fee payable. (Closed Christmas Day to mid January).

Starting Point locator map for Walks 11-21

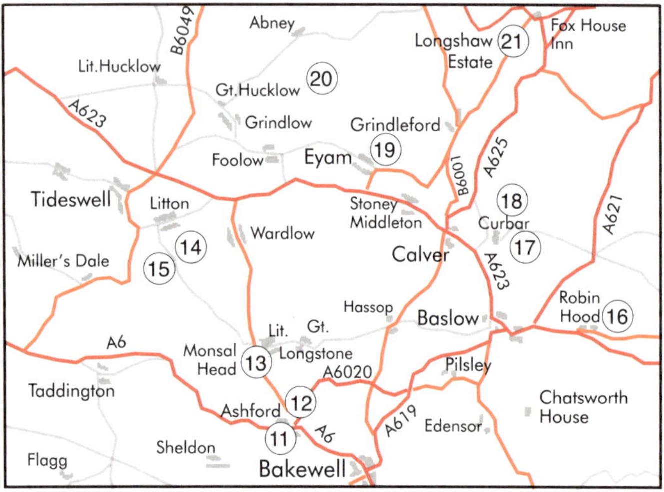

Walk	Title	Starting Point	Grid Reference	Page
11	Magpie Mine	Ashford-in-the-Water	SK19446976	62
12	Headstone Tunnel	Ashford-in-the-Water	SK19446976	66

Directions: From the A6, take the turning onto the A6020. Then take the first turn left, signed 'B6465' into Ashford-in-the-Water. After the church the road bends right. In about 150 yards the small car park is signed to the right. Free parking. Toilets. (Also parking in the lay-by near the bend).

Walk	Title	Starting Point	Grid Reference	Page
13	Monsal Dale	Monsal Head	SK18517152	70

Directions: As above, but take the first right on entering Ashford-in-the-Water, signed 'Monsal Head, Wardlow' (still the B6465). In about a mile, turn left into the 'long stay' pay-and-display car park. Public toilets. Also roadside parking along the road to the right (signed 'Little Longstone').

Walk	Title	Starting Point	Grid Reference	Page
14	Miller's Dale	Cressbrook Mill	SK17337267	74
15	Cressbrook Dale	Cressbrook Mill	SK17337267	78

Directions: As above but turn left after Monsal Head car park. Go past a pub and café at Monsal Head and the road bends sharp right downhill. In about 1/2 mile ignore the car park on the left. Keep straight on and in another 1/2 mile there is ample roadside parking on either side, adjacent to the former Cressbrook Mill.

Directions to parking locations and relevant information

Walk	Title	Starting Point	Grid Reference	Page
16	Gardom's Edge	Birchen Edge car park	SK28027214	82

Directions: Birchen Edge car park is in the area known as Robin Hood. It is off the A619, 5 miles west of Chesterfield. Turn onto the B6050, signed 'Cutthorpe, Whittington.' (Sign not visible from the Chesterfield direction). The free car park is just beyond the entrance to the Robin Hood Inn.

Walk	Title	Starting Point	Grid Reference	Page
17	Curbar Edge	Curbar Gap car park	SK26217471	86
18	Baslow Edge	Curbar Gap car park	SK26217471	90

Directions: From the A623, about $1\frac{1}{4}$ miles north of Baslow take the turning on the right to Curbar. Continue through the village up the hill. At the top Curbar Gap car park is on the left. Pay-and-display (free for National Trust members). Or access from the A621 to the east.

Walk	Title	Starting Point	Grid Reference	Page
19	Eyam & Riley Gr.	Eyam car park	SK21667669	92

Directions: From the A623, $\frac{3}{4}$ mile west of Stoney Middleton. Take the B6521 signed 'Eyam.' At the top of the hill bear left. Go past the church and Eyam Hall, then take the first right at the car park sign (Hawkhill Road). Go past the entrance to the first car park (pay-and-display) and take the next right into the free car park (but donations welcome), kindly provided by Eyam Parish Council. The walk starts from this car park. Note closing times - April to September-8pm. Oct to March-5pm.

Walk	Title	Starting Point	Grid Reference	Page
20	Bretton Clough	SIr William Hill Road	SK21027775	96

From the A623 (Baslow direction) turn right at Calver crossroads, signed 'Froggatt, Sheffield A625.' In 300 yards ignore the right turn 'A625.' Keep straight on. At Grindleford in $1\frac{3}{4}$ miles turn sharp left, signed 'Hathersage B6001.' The road bends right, with Sir William Hotel on the right. Turn sharp left opposite the Hotel onto the steep Sir William Hill Road. After $1\frac{1}{4}$ miles the road bends sharply to the left. Keep on the road and turn right in $\frac{1}{2}$ mile, signed 'Great Hucklow, Bretton.' In 1 mile the road bends sharp left. Park on the right-hand verge just before the bend.

Walk	Title	Starting Point	Grid Reference	Page
21	Longshaw Estate	Woodcroft car park	SK 26658006	100

Directions: From the A623, turn onto the A625. In about 300 yards turn right, signed 'Froggatt, Sheffield A625.' In $1\frac{1}{2}$ miles turn left at the junction with the B6054. Ignore a road to the right. The Woodcroft, National Trust car park is signed to the left, about 150 yards before the junction with the A6187. Pay-and-display (free for National Trust members).

Walk 1 ~ Crich Chase and Cromford Canal 3 3/4 miles

Start: Market Place, Crich. Free.
GR: SK34975419. **Map:** OS Exp. OL24.
Distance: 3 3/4 miles (6.0 km).
Allow: 2 1/2 hours.
Terrain: Field paths, woodland, canal towpath. A short steep uphill and then the last 3/4 mile is a more gradual ascent.
Public toilets: Crich (just off-route - above the Black Swan Inn).
Refreshments: Pub and chip shop in Crich.
Summary of the Walk: On leaving Crich, there are lovely views along the Derwent Valley, before the route descends through the attractive woodland of Crich Chase. It then continues to join the Cromford Canal following the towpath for 3/4 mile. The canal isn't used by boats and is a tranquil haven for walkers and wildlife alike. Leaving the towpath, the final mile is an ascent across fields back up to Crich.
Maximum height: 640ft (195m). **Ascent:** 394ft (120m)

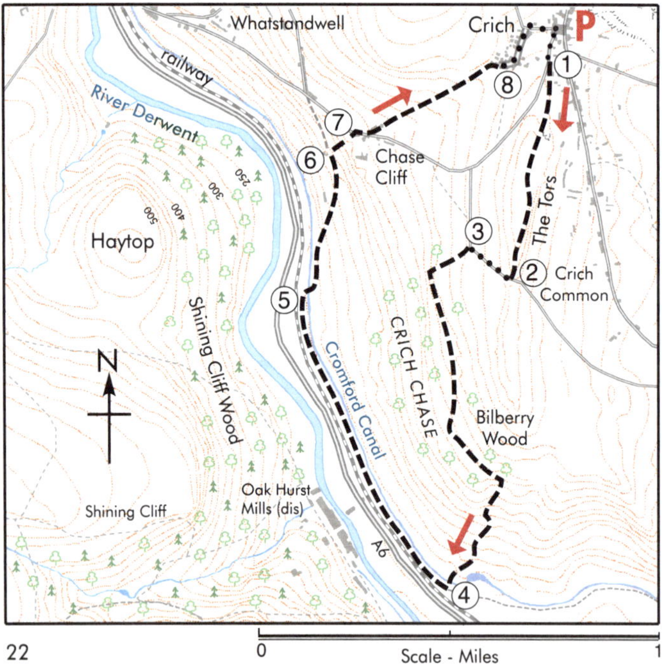

Directions ~ Crich Chase and Cromford Canal Walk 1

From the Market Place parking area, walk along the road, just to the right of the imposing stone building, the Baptist Chapel. This is Sandy Lane. Ignore a path to the left after 100 yards.

① In another 45 yards bear left at a sign, 'Derwent Valley walk,' go up steps to reach trees circled by a wall, with the word 'Jubilee' on it. Look for a date carved in one of the stones. It was done to commemorate Queen Victoria's Golden Jubilee. Look over the wall just beyond the enclosure. Running below was a railway built by George Stephenson. It was opened in 1841 to transport limestone from local quarries to kilns at Cromford Canal below. It was used until 1957. On a clear day you should be able to see steam rising from the cooling towers of the power stations along the Trent Valley, to the east. Continue on to another tree enclosure. Look for another date carved in a stone. This commemorates Queen Victoria's Diamond Jubilee. Go through the stile, signed 'Chadwick Nick.' An enclosed path leads to another stile. Go through, following the path running alongside a wall. The path crosses fields, you go over two step-stiles and then on to a squeeze stile. Go through, keeping to the wall, ignoring a path running downhill to a gate. Then turn left, through a stile at a yellow arrow. Walk down steps to a lane.

② Turn right along the lane for 250 yards, to reach a path on the left.

③ Turn left through a stile, signed 'public footpath,' the path runs alongside the wall. In 250 yards go over a stile (or through gap), and turn left. In 150 yards you enter woodland. The species of trees you may see include chestnut, oak, silver birch, beech, sycamore and holly. Birds that might be seen are jay, great-spotted woodpecker and nuthatch.

Keep straight on, along a path marked occasionally with yellow arrows. In just under 1/2 mile you reach a small open grassy area. At the end keep straight on ignoring a path bearing left and one to the right. The path descends and bends right passing between old stone gateposts. In 150 yards keep straight on to an arrowed post to descend a sunken track. Worn deep by hundreds of years of use. In about 1/4 mile pass through a gateway, emerging from the woods to descend a grass slope.

④ Go through the gate. To the left is a sunken water trough. Turn right going over the canal bridge. Turn right at the end of the bridge down to

Walk 1 ~ Crich Chase and Cromford Canal 3 3/4 miles

	Grid references	miles
P	SK3497954196	0.00
①	SK3493254082	0.10
②	SK3481553228	0.68
③	SK3463053355	0.82
④	SK3453152057	1.83
⑤	SK3395353161	2.66
⑥	SK3406653722	3.04
⑦	SK3415053788	3.12
⑧	SK3478654034	3.62

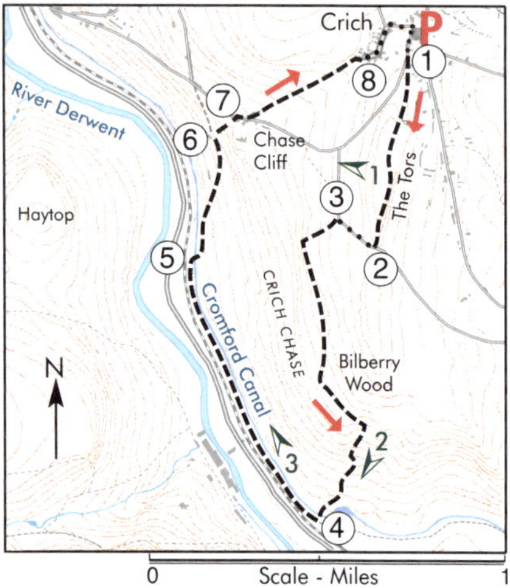

1 Derwent Valley, from The Tors

2 frosted leaves, Crich Chase

3 Cromford Canal

the canal towpath. Bear left, the canal to your right. Cromford Canal was completed in 1794, it was 14 miles long, and linked the cotton mills and other industries in the area with the Erewash Canal, and other parts of the country. It closed in 1944. Running alongside the canal is a railway, opened in 1849. You'll also notice the River Derwent flowing parallel with the railway and the busy A6 road. You pass a building. Note the barn type doors, facing the canal. It may have been used for goods storage. In just under 1/4 mile is another house. Note the date carved into the end. Continue on the towpath. You will probably see mallards, moorhens, coots and little grebes (dabchick) along here. If you're very lucky, you may even see the electric-blue flash of a kingfisher. Water voles also live along here, the canal is managed to encourage wildlife.

5. After about 1/2 mile just before a bridge, bear left, leaving the canal. Then turn right, crossing the bridge. In 15 yards turn left at an arrow into woodland. The path runs into a walled lane, going uphill. Continue past a farm entrance on the left. In 150 yards ignore a housing entrance to the left. In another 100 yards you pass a cottage and a garage. Then in about 40 yards look for an arrowed post to the right at a wall corner.

6. Turn right here and follow the path as it climbs steeply alongside the wall. In 140 yards you reach a road junction.

7. Go through the stile, bear right and walk away from the corner before crossing with care. In about 100 yards, turn left at a footpath sign. Keep straight on and at the end of the track go over a stile. Follow the path straight on as it runs upwards alongside the wall. At the end of the second field, go through the gateway, following the path alongside the left hand wall. In 50 yards ignore the green metal gate on the left. Keep straight on and in about 150 yards go through a stile at a metal gate and walk straight on. Follow a track between houses, which leads to a road. Bear right along the road through the housing area.

8. In about 60 yards it bends sharply left, keep on the road ignoring avenues off. Where the road widens at the junction, bear right downhill, joining the road descending back to the Market Place. At the Market Place you'll see a long stone water trough divided into sections. This dates to the days when horses were the main form of transport.

Walk 2 ~ Crich Memorial 4 1/2 miles

Start: Market Place, Crich. **GR:** SK34975419.
Map: OL24. **Distance:** 4 1/2 miles (7.2 km).
Allow: 3 hours.
Terrain: Fields, lanes, canal path, woodland. There is a mile of uphill as the route leaves the canal and climbs back up towards Crich.
Public toilets: In Crich, on the road above the Black Swan Inn.
Refreshments: Pub in Crich. Café at Crich Memorial (not Mon. or Wed.)
Summary of the Walk: From Crich, the route gains height, giving expansive views along the Derwent Valley, before a stepped descent through the hamlet of Crich Carr. It then leads through an old quarry, now wooded and reclaimed by nature. Emerging from the woods it follows the Cromford Canal, before climbing up to Cliff Quarry and the Crich Memorial. (The Memorial Tower has great views from the top. It is open every day, except Christmas Day, Boxing Day, New Year's Day. 10am - 5pm, 4pm winter, subject to weather conditions. Admission is free, but donations welcome). From there the route follows fields and roads back to Crich village.
Maximum height: 938ft (286m).
Ascent: 659ft (201m).

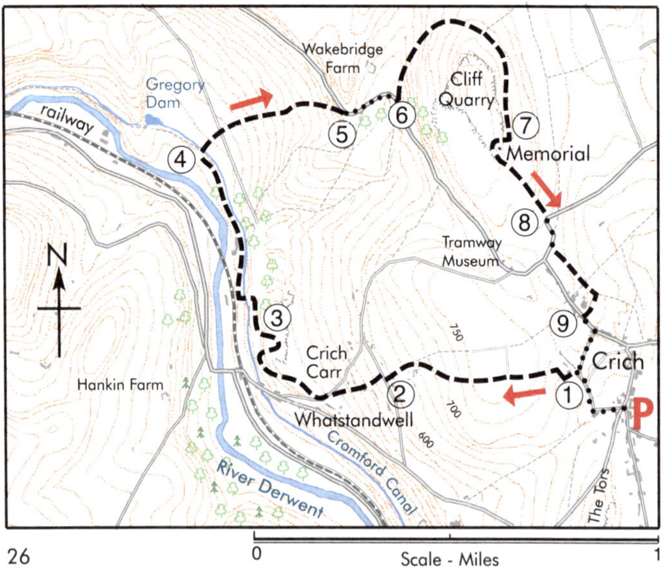

To orientate yourself in the Market Place parking area, walk up the road with your back to the shops. In about 150 yards at the sign for 'Bulling Lane,' turn right up 'Coasthill.' In about 100 yards on the right, look out for a small bridge. This is one of the few remaining fragments of a railway that used to run from the quarries locally, down to Cromford Canal. It was built in 1841 and closed in 1957. Keep straight on. Ignore Jeffries Lane to the right and Wheatsheaf Lane to the right. Carry on up to reach the end of the road. There is a wide track left and one straight on.

(1) Take the left track, signed 'public footpath,' it bends sharp right in about 35 yards and then shortly turns left, going up between hedges. (This may be overgrown with nettles in late summer). At the end go through the stile into a field. Follow the narrow path along the field, a wall to the left. In about 250 yards the path bears right to a wall and stile. Go through and walk straight on, with old farm buildings to your left. Then go through another stile and descend to an unsurfaced lane. Cross over and go down a steep, stepped path, which leads to a road.

(2) Turn right along the road for 20 yards, then turn left at a sign for 'Whatstandwell.' The path descends and leads to a lane between houses. Continue straight on and in about 100 yards bear left, signed by a yellow arrow on a telegraph pole at a right-hand bend. Walk down the lane and in about 80 yards you'll reach a junction. Bear left here, continuing downhill. In about 50 yards, turn right just before a derelict chapel, onto a wide path. (It is signed on the opposite side of the road 'Robin Hood'). Where the car track bends right, keep straight on. You'll pass some allotments to your right. Keep straight on, ignoring gates either side, until you reach the end of the path. Go through the gate into woodland. In about 130 yards the path bends sharply right. (At the corner ignore a narrow path leaving steeply left). Keep on the now wider path as it bends right and descends. In about 80 yards, with an old quarry face ahead, the path bends sharp left up a wooded valley.

(3) In about 200 yards you reach a road. Cross over and walk along the wide path diagonally opposite. In 150 yards, turn left at a sign post and go over a canal bridge. Then turn right to the canal. Turn left along the towpath. In about 1/2 mile the canal goes beneath a bridge. At the far

Walk 2 ~ Crich Memorial 4 1/2 miles

	Grid references	miles
P	SK3497954196	0.00
①	SK3476754369	0.20
②	SK3386954340	0.80
③	SK3325254550	1.39
④	SK3303155358	1.96
⑤	SK3370655499	2.49
⑥	SK3393955571	2.66
⑦	SK3445055490	3.50
⑧	SK3463655014	3.85
⑨	SK3480454615	4.19

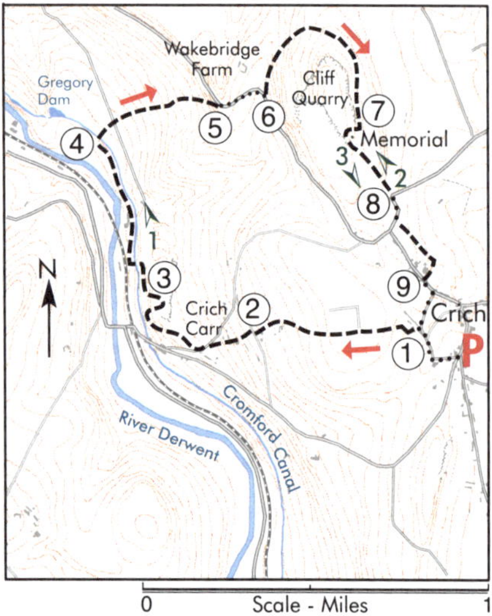

1 winter reflections, Cromford Canal

2 Crich, from the Memorial

3 Crich Memorial

side, turn left immediately, going up steps.

(4) Go through a gate, turn left over the canal bridge and along a driveway, past a house. At the road junction, cross over and go straight on, signed 'Leashaw.' The track passes a house and then goes up into woodland. In 1/3 mile the wood ends, go through a gate and alongside a fence.

(5) Go over a stile at the road and turn right. In 150 yards pass the track to a farm (opposite), in another 150 yards the road bends right. Cross over where safe, before the bend. Then on the left is a wide gravel track, having signs for 'Cliff Farm, Caravan Club Site.' Also a 'footpath' sign.

(6) Turn left here along the track. In 220 yards, with a large house ahead, bear right uphill, signed by an arrow. Go through a gate. In about 100 yards, ignore a path to the left, continue uphill signed 'Crich' and through another gate. The path then leads across the tram lines of the Crich Tramway Museum. Continue straight on, the wire fencing of a quarry to your right. In about 200 yards ignore a path to the left, keep on the path alongside the wire fence. In about 1/4 mile is a stile.

(7) Go through the stile and in about 10 yards turn right, up a narrow path to reach a triangular pillar. From the trig. point walk down to the right of the tall tower. It is locally called Crich Stand. It is a memorial to commemorate the soldiers of the Sherwood Foresters Regiment who died in the two World Wars. Look at the inscribed stone tablet above the entrance. Notice how it gives the date of the First World War as 1914-1919, when the date above reads 1914-1918. This is because the war ended on the Armistice, 11th November 1918, but the peace treaty, the Versailles Treaty, was not signed until 28th June1919. Go up the tower for great views. Walk down the straight wide path to the road junction.

(8) Cross over and turn right along the road. In about 120 yards, turn left at a footpath sign. Ignore the path sharp left, keep straight on towards the church. Follow the path over three fields, then go through a gate signed 'Roes Lane.' Go through a graveyard, at the end turn right on the lane.

(9) At the main road cross over and turn left. In about 70 yards, turn right down a narrow lane at the side of a house. In about 220 yards you reach the end of Wheatsheaf Lane. Bear left here, retracing outward steps descending the road back to the Market Place.

Walk 3 ~ High Peak Junction — 3 3/4 miles

Start: High Peak Junction, Pay & display.
GR: SK31544610. **Map:** OS Exp. OL24.
Distance: 3 3/4 miles (6.0 km).
Allow: 2 hours.
Terrain: Mainly surfaced tracks - rail trackbeds and canal towpaths. Just one uphill section along the trackbed of the disused railway incline.
Public toilets: At High Peak Junction and Cromford Wharf.
Refreshments: At High Peak Junction and Cromford Wharf.
Summary of the Walk: A walk through the relics and reminders of our industrial transport history. The walk follows the Cromford Canal, passing the impressive chimney of Leawood Pumphouse, and continues on to High Peak Junction. Here there is a visitor's centre and light refreshments are available. The next section is up an incline, once part of the Cromford and High Peak Railway, now the High Peak Trail. Leaving the Trail the route descends a walled track, with impressive views along the valley towards Matlock. The final section rejoins the Cromford Canal for about a mile.
Maximum Height: 607ft (185m). **Ascent:** 311ft (95m).

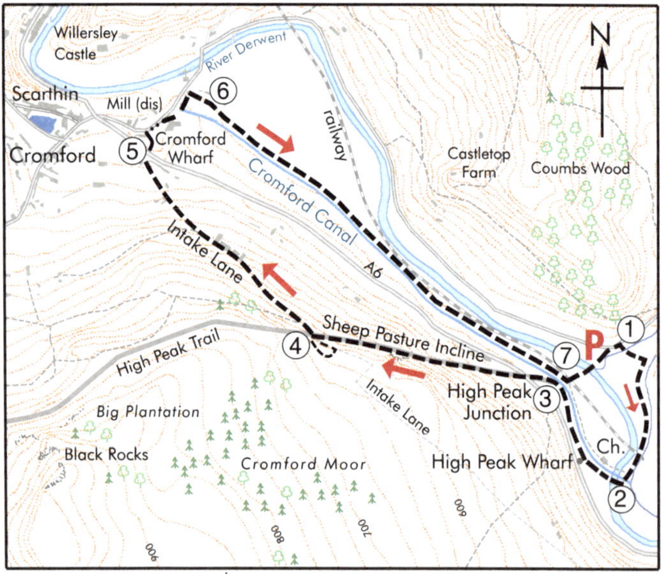

0 — Scale - Miles — 1

Leave the car park by the far corner. Go up the steps, turn left and at the path junction turn left. (High Peak Junction is signed to the right).

(1) At the road, turn right. In about 75 yards, turn right on a rough road between houses (the footpath sign is on the opposite side of the road). In about 25 yards, turn left at a 'footpath turn left' sign onto a path by a stream. After about 100 yards, turn right at the junction with a wide track. Note the overgrown channel to your left. This was the Leawood Branch of the Cromford Canal and was used to transport goods to the nearby Lea Mills. After about 330 yards you cross a footbridge over a railway. In a further 150 yards you reach a canal. This is the Cromford Canal, completed in 1794. It was 14 miles long and linked up with the Erewash Canal. Coal, limestone and cotton were the main materials that were transported. It was in use until 1944. Look to your left to see a derelict building. This is a lengthman's cottage, built around 1830. A lengthman was responsible for the maintenance of a measured section of canal. Cross the bridge to the other side of the canal.

(2) Turn right along the canal. A bridge carries it high above the River Derwent. This is an aqueduct. 'Aqua' is latin for water and 'duct' comes from the latin 'ducere' which means to lead. As you walk on, the impressive chimney is part of Leawood Pumphouse. Opened in 1849, it was used to pump water from the River Derwent into the canal to replenish the level, ensuring boats could continue to operate. It still occasionally operates and you can see it working on special 'steaming days.' When opposite the building the path bears left to a junction. Turn right signed 'Cromford.' You now go through the site of the former High Peak Wharf, now a residential centre. You pass beneath a white metal arch. What do you think it is for? Where you're standing used to be a rail waggon yard. The arch is a loading gauge. No goods could be any higher than this, as it is set at the height of the lowest bridge on the railway. Further on is a white pillar which was the base of a crane used for lifting goods from narrowboats onto the waggons. In about 300 yards you reach the old workshops of the High Peak Junction. This is where the Cromford and High Peak Railway joined the Cromford Canal. It opened in 1831 and ran 33 3/4 miles to Whaley Bridge, linking with the Peak Forest Canal.

Walk 3 ~ High Peak Junction 3 3/4 miles

	Grid references	miles
P	SK3147756097	0.00
①	SK3153756098	0.06
②	SK3162855602	0.49
③	SK3136255984	0.86
④	SK3041656153	1.50
⑤	SK2979956856	2.26
⑥	SK3000657027	2.49
⑦	SK3136356020	3.54

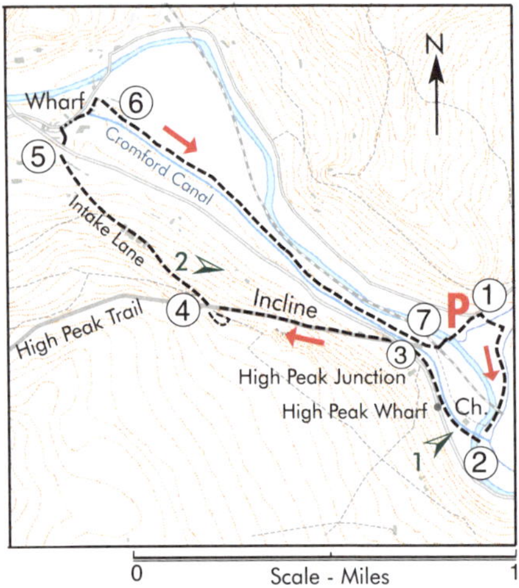

2 across the valley

High Peak Junction

1 Leawood Pumphouse

(3) Turn left, walking between the building and the railway waggons. In a pit just after the waggons note the large pulley which controlled the cable. Loaded waggons were hauled up the incline by cable. Walk on up the incline through a tunnel. 100 yards beyond, in the middle of the trackbed is a sloping pit. This was a 'catch pit' constructed to stop runaway waggons ending up in the canal. Have a look in. After 1/3 mile, on the left are the scant remains of the Cromford Incline winding engine. This operated between 1837 and 1857. After 1857 the Cromford Incline was combined with Sheep Pasture Incline, the latter name being retained. It is 1,320 yards long and waggons were hauled by a steam winding engine at the top of the incline. The railway closed in 1967.

(4) In a further 1/4 mile there is a footpath sign to the left. Turn left here, following the yellow arrows. Ignore the stile to the right and descend to a path junction. Turn left at the sign for 'Cromford.' The wide track goes back under the Incline. In about 60 yards, ignore the footpath slanting left. Keep on the main track. In 1/5 mile the track becomes a road at the outskirts of Cromford. The road descends for about 1/3 mile. At the bottom walk on the right-hand side to a junction with the main road.

(5) Cross over the busy road and go through the gap in the wall opposite. At the driveway, turn left to reach a road. Turn right, keeping on the right-hand side. Sir Richard Arkwright's Cromford Mill is opposite. This was built in 1771 as a water-powered cotton-spinning mill. In about 170 yards you reach a building at Cromford Wharf. This is where boats carrying raw cotton were unloaded and loaded back up with processed yarn from the mill. Keep straight on, the building to your right. At the far corner of the last building turn right. Walk alongside it and keep straight on for about 30 yards. Go up the steps from the car park to the canal.

(6) Walk along the towpath, the canal to your right. The path is called a towpath because prior to engines powering narrowboats, they were towed by horses. Keep on the towpath and in just over a mile you'll again see the buildings of High Peak Junction across the canal.

(7) Turn left at the path crossroads, signed 'car park and Lea Bridge.' Walk over the footbridge above the railway and in about 150 yards go across the river bridge. Then in a few yards turn left back into the car park.

Walk 4 ~ High Tor, Matlock Bath — 3 3/4 miles

Start: Artist Corner car park, near Matlock. Pay-and-display. **GR:** SK29715955.
Map: OS Exp. OL24.
Distance: 3 3/4 miles (6.0 km). **Allow:** 2 1/2 hours.
Terrain: Mainly surfaced paths, but some sections may be muddy. There are unfenced cliff edges at High Tor. Children must be kept under close supervision.
Public toilets: At the car park and in Hall Leys Park, Matlock.
Refreshments: Various pubs and cafés in Matlock Bath and Matlock.
Summary of the Walk: A gradual ascent to reach the viewpoint of High Tor. Descending from High Tor the walk reaches Matlock Bath. From here there is a fairly steep ascent on a road (with pavement). The route then follows a path passing beneath the Heights of Abraham. Finally there are great views before a descent into Matlock. A path alongside the River Derwent leads back to the car park.
Maximum Height: 672 ft (205 m). **Ascent:** 640 ft (195 m).

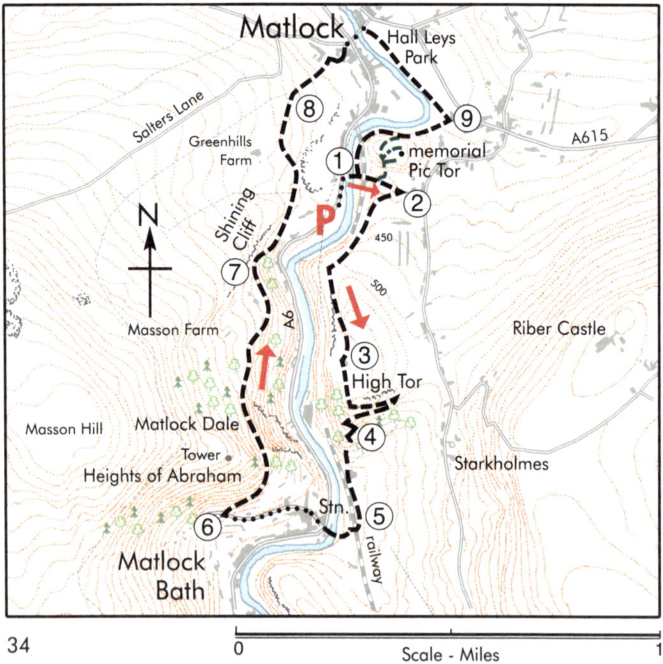

Leave the car park by the far corner (away from the toilet block).

① Turn right and in 120 yards turn right over the footbridge to cross the river. Walk straight on going under a bridge, signed 'High Tor,' going uphill. In about 50 yards ignore a path left signed 'War Memorial Pic Tor.' In another 100 yards there is a path to the left.

② Turn sharp right here, going beneath an overhead sign 'High Tor Grounds.' The High Tor pleasure grounds were a fashionable place for the Victorians. In the 1860s new paths were made, linking the two resorts of Matlock and Matlock Bath. (See the information board). Walk up the wide path, passing two viewpoints on the right. Ensure you keep close control of children and dogs, as there is a cliff to the right. The ruins on the hill to the left are the remains of Riber Castle, built in the 1860s for John Smedley, a local mill owner. In just under 1/2 mile, keep straight on across the grass area, then on to an information board.

③ Turn right here and in 8 yards continue straight on, up the stepped path, ignoring a path left. This leads up to a grassy knoll with great views and unfenced sheer edges. You must keep close supervision of children and keep dogs on a lead. Don't trip - stop to look at the views. You now have a choice. The path bearing left goes to the summit of High Tor. Alternatively you can take what is called the 'Giddy Edge,' path. It is signed as such. This is a 'one-way' path following a ledge (not too narrow!) girdling High Tor. It gives great views into and along the valley. **If you take the Giddy Edge path** - at the end you come to a path junction. Cross this and go straight on (just to the right of a tree) to follow a narrow path between fences. The path gives views down into the adjacent deep lead rakes. Lead was mined here for hundreds of years, maybe even during the Roman occupation about 1,700 years ago.

If you take the path over High Tor summit - Just after the top is a bench seat. About 20 yards down from here is a tree on the left. Turn left here along a narrow path between fences. At the end, turn right on the wide tarmac path. The path then bends left as it descends. 20 yards after the bend there is a path on the right (opposite a bench seat).

④ Turn sharp right here along the stepped zig-zag path downhill. At the bottom pass beneath the 'High Tor Grounds.' Turn right on the wide

Walk 4 ~ High Tor, Matlock Bath 3 3/4 miles

	Grid references	miles
P	SK2971259555	0.00
1	SK2973559677	0.07
2	SK2992559635	0.17
3	SK2972159014	0.68
4	SK2976758826	0.91
5	SK2977258431	1.30
6	SK2920258451	1.69
7	SK2939859276	2.31
8	SK2956559998	2.82
9	SK3009459867	3.31

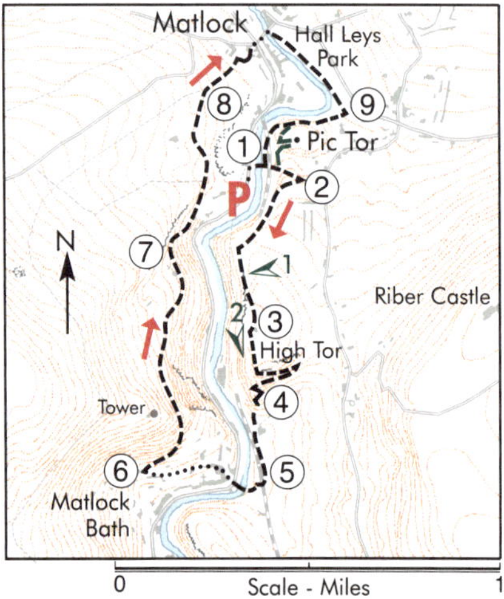

≺ 1 View from High Tor

≺ 2 Giddy Edge, High Tor

Memorial, Pic Tor

path past the cable car station. Go through the stile at a gate and in 15 yards, bear left signed 'Railway Station, Lovers Walk.'

(5) In 200 yards cross the rail line at the crossing point. Then walk straight on, and in 90 yards bear right, signed 'Village Centre.' Cross the bridge to reach the main road. Cross over with care (if busy use the pedestrian crossing to the left). Walk straight on up the road opposite (Holme Road). Ignore roads to the right, keep going uphill. In about 1/4 mile at the top the road bends left at a junction (letterbox in the wall). Keep on Upperwood Road. (Ignore Waterloo Road to the left). In 250 yards there is a footpath on the right, signed 'Matlock.'

(6) Turn right here, passing through woodland. In 1/2 mile at a junction with a wide track, bear right downhill. In 180 yards is a road junction.

(7) Turn right going downhill passing a converted chapel in about 150 yards. At the end of the building bear left on a footpath. This path keeps mainly on the level. In 1/4 mile go straight on at a path crossroads. In 200 yards go through a stile on the right and straight on over fields.

(8) In about 270 yards at the prominent signpost and path junction, turn right downhill towards Matlock. Note the large building on the hillside opposite. This used to be 'Smedley's Hydro,' built in 1886 by John Smedley. Patrons arrived by train and were transported up the hill by horse-drawn trams to 'take the waters.' At the bottom of the field go through a stile and down the road, signed 'Limestone Way.' At the junction with a main road, turn right and cross over. At the bottom use the two pedestrian crossings and walk over the bridge. After the bridge turn right into the park, following a straight path alongside the river. After 1/3 mile, at the end of the park, go straight on at the road for 12 yards.

(9) Then turn right at a sign 'Pic Tor and Knowleston Gardens.' Go over a footbridge and turn right. The path follows the river again. In about 320 yards there is sign 'War Memorial.' To visit the memorial (at Pic Tor) adds 1/4 mile. To do so turn left here, going up for 1/5 mile. Walk past the memorial keeping to the path, which then descends. Take two left turns on the descent. At the junction turn right under the bridge and retrace steps to the car park. Otherwise keep on the riverside path. At the junction turn right over the bridge. Retrace steps to the car park.

Walk 5 ~ Stanton Moor 2 miles

Start: Informal lay-bys on the Birchover to Stanton-in-Peak road. Alternative parking at Birchover Stone Quarry (free public parking in the lower section).

GR: 24196280 (lay-by). **Map:** OS Exp. OL24.

Distance: 2 miles. (3.2 km). **Allow:** 1¼ hours.

Terrain: Well-defined paths throughout. Sometimes stony but mainly grassy or sandy. Not muddy even in winter. Mainly level. Two step-stiles.

Public toilets: None, but public toilets nearby in Birchover.

Refreshments: None, but two pubs in Birchover.

Summary of the Walk: A short walk but full of interest and with great views. Stanton Moor is a last remaining remnant of moorland, in this area, which would have once been extensive. The walk is mainly on the level, passing several interesting features notably the Cork Stone and the Nine Ladies Stone Circle. The area has many archaeological remains, tumuli, stone circles and earthworks. There are some fine views along Darley Dale as the route follows the edge of the moor.

Maximum Height: 1080ft (329m). **Ascent:** 130ft (39m).

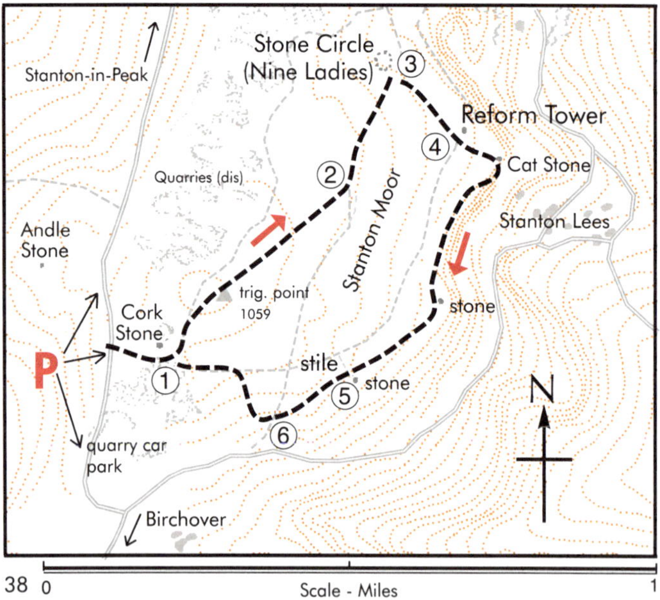

From your chosen parking spot, walk along the road to the footpath sign, and the two big notices about Stanton Moor. Walk along the path and in about 50 yards go through a gate and follow the slightly rising stony track. After 120 yards you come to the first interesting feature of the walk. The large upright stone to the left is called the Cork Stone. A little imagination is needed to see that it roughly resembles a bottle's cork stopper, narrower at the bottom and wider at the top. The scooped out steps and the iron hoops inserted in the 19th century, make it an easy climb. Be careful though if you go up, and take extra care coming down not to miss your step. Descending is always more difficult than going up.

(1) Bear left just after the stone and follow the path alongside a disused quarry. In about 50 yards near the end of the quarry, take the right-hand fork in the path, going gently uphill along a grassy path. In 150 yards you reach the highest point of the moor, (1059ft, 323m) marked with a trig. point. There are lovely panoramic views from here over the surrounding lower countryside. Keep a look out - the moor contains many archaeological features dating back to the Bronze Age, there are a number of tumuli - little raised mounds, earthworks and pits, which may have been used for burials or other aspects of Bronze Age life. Continue on the path across the moorland, as it descends to a junction with a wider track.

(2) Turn left here and in about 300 yards you enter an area of birch woodland. Ahead and to the left you'll see a circle of small stones. Continue on the main path to reach an information board. The folklore is that nine ladies were turned to stone for dancing on the Sabbath. Hence Nine Ladies Stone Circle. Just to the southwest is another larger stone, the King Stone which represents the fiddle player. It is thought the circle and many of the other archaeological remains on the moor were constructed about 1500BC, in the Bronze Age, or earlier. No one really knows why they were made, but it is likely they were places of worship and ritual. Have a wander around and then retrace your steps to the information board. Now stand with your back to the board.

(3) Go straight on, crossing the main path and follow a sandy path. In about 180 yards at a fork in the path, keep straight on, ignoring the

Walk 5 ~ Stanton Moor 2 miles

	Grid references	miles
P	SK2419162800	0.00
①	SK2435062785	0.11
②	SK2482263191	0.53
③	SK2493763478	0.73
④	SK2512563396	0.88
⑤	SK2482462735	1.52
⑥	SK2462362637	1.66

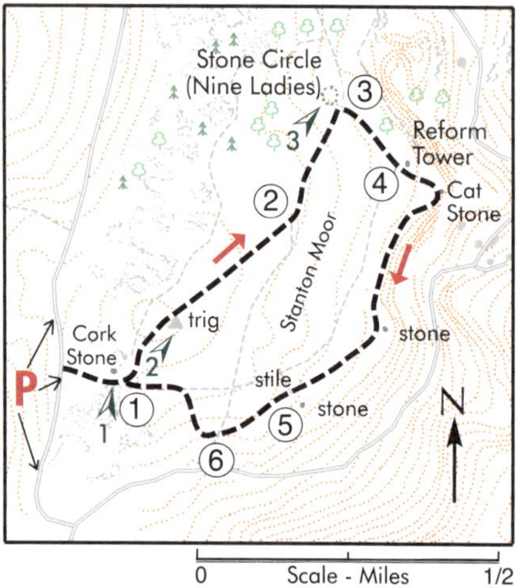

1 Cork Stone, Stanton Moor

2 triangulation point, Stanton Moor

3 strange shadows, Nine Ladies Stone Circle, Stanton Moor

path veering right. You will shortly come to a square granite tower, the Reform Tower or Earl Grey Tower. Over the door there used to be a carved stone tablet, 'Earl Grey 1832.' It was built in honour of Charles Grey, 2nd Earl Grey and a Whig Prime Minister. His name lives on at our tea tables in Earl Grey tea. The tea should really be named 'Lady Grey,' as it was she who had the distinctive tea blended. It wasn't patented so the family has never made any money from it. Earl Grey's contribution to society was to persuade a reluctant Parliament to pass The Representation of the People Act 1832, more commonly known as the The Reform Act 1832. This created a fairer, more representative system of electing MPs and eliminated the so-called 'rotten boroughs.' The tower was built on the instruction of William Thornhill of Stanton Hall.

④ Go over the stile at the tower and turn right, the narrow path descends to join a wider track. Walk with a wire fence to your right. In about 250 yards the path bends sharp right at the fence corner. Walk straight on for a short diversion to another notable rock, the Cat Stone. It has hand and foot holds scooped into it and is easy to climb, but take great care if you do. Retrace your steps to the fence corner and turn sharp left, walking with the fence to your right. There are great views along this next section along Darley Dale, towards Matlock, Riber Castle and beyond. Just a short way off the path to the left, there are one or two rocky viewpoints which make convenient picnic points. Continue along the path and in just under 1/2 mile is another large rock and a National Trust sign 'Stanton Moor Edge.' To the right is a step-stile in the fence.

⑤ Go over the stile. An information board tells that the track along the edge of the moor was known as Duke's Drive. The area was once owned by the Duke of Rutland, who used to entertain guests with horse-drawn scenic carriage rides. Turn left, and continue straight on ignoring the path to the right. In 270 yards you reach a slanting crossroads at a wide track.

⑥ Go straight on along a narrow grassy path. This meanders through a long-abandoned quarry. It gains height to meet a wide track. Turn left along the wide track and you shortly reach the Cork Stone. Continue straight on, the stone to your right to retrace steps back to the road.

Walk 6 ~ Lathkill Dale (east) 4 3/4 miles

Start: Lay-bys on both sides of the road in Alport. **GR:** SK21966458. **Map:** OS Exp. OL24.
Distance: 4 3/4 miles (7.6 km). **Allow:** 2 1/2 hours.
Terrain: Good paths along the dales. A short road section. Field paths. Several step-stiles. The path at Meadow Place Grange is usually very muddy. Cows and bullocks in some fields.
Public toilets: In Youlgrave, slightly off the route.
Refreshments: Three pubs in Youlgrave.
Summary of the Walk: From Alport the walk follows a crystal clear trout river along Bradford Dale. The route leaves the dale and passes through Youlgrave. A gradual ascent on a lane leads to a walled track, then fields to reach Meadow Place Grange. After leaving here a track winds down through woodland into Lathkill Dale. The final section follows the beautiful riverside path down to Conksbury Bridge and on into Alport.
Maximum height: 794 ft (242 m). **Ascent:** 390 ft (119 m).

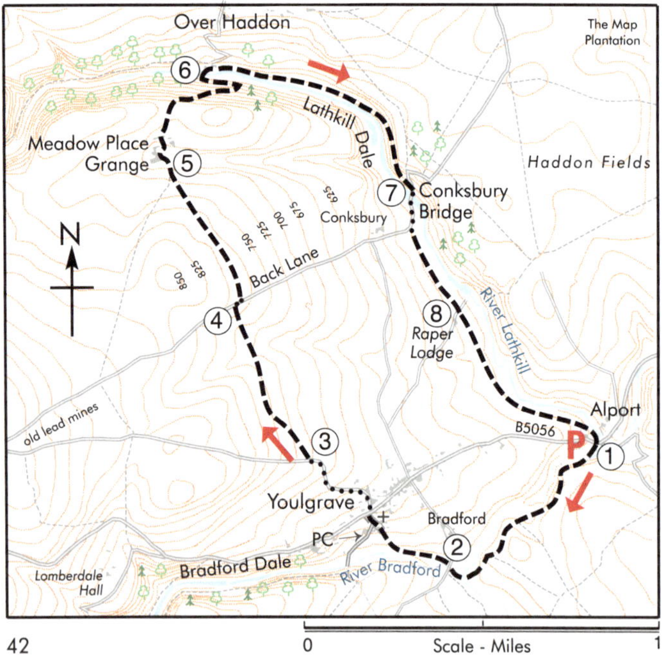

From the lay-by walk down the hill to the phone box and the river.

1. Turn right at the phone box, signed 'footpath,' along a tarmac track. Go through a gate, following the riverside path along Bradford Dale. In about 1/4 mile go through a stile (or gate), then in about 90 yards you have the option of bearing right away from the track to keep near the river. Or keep on the track. Either way you soon pass a little arched bridge. Keep by the river and in 250 yards you reach a gate at a road. Another choice here, either go straight along the right-hand side of the river to the gate, or more interestingly, bear left over the river and then immediately right. Pass a seat and then cross the slab footbridge over the river to the gate.

2. Go through the gate and along the riverside path. In about 150 yards bear right, leaving the riverside path and going up the slanting path up the dale side, towards Youlgrave. After passing through a stile a walled track leads to a road. Keep straight on up the road and at the junction bear right. (For the toilets turn left down the hill for 100 yards). Keep on the right-hand side, passing a chapel to reach the main road. If you wish to explore Youlgrave - walk to the right for All Saint's Church with its altar window designed by the Pre-Raphaelite artist Edward Burne-Jones. Opposite the church is the George Hotel. If you walk to the left there are two more pubs and a distinctive fountain. Indeed Youlgrave has its own independent water company - Youlgrave Waterworks Ltd.
Cross over, turn right and in a few yards turn left up Moor Lane. Then at the slanting junction, bear left continuing uphill (still on Moor Lane). In about 300 yards you pass a 'Quiet Lane' sign. This is to make drivers aware that the lane is used by walkers, cyclists and horse-riders.

3. In another 200 yards at a left-hand bend, bear right and follow a walled track at a footpath sign. In 1/4 mile the walled section ends. Go through the gate, continue straight on (more or less parallel with a broken wall to your left). In 200 yards descend to a gate in a wire fence. Go through and walk straight on up the field. (Again parallel to the wall on the left). In 1/4 mile you reach the top of the field at a wall.

4. Go through two stiles in succession onto the road. Turn right and in about 50 yards turn left, over a stile at a sign 'Over Haddon 1.' The path

Walk 6 ~ Lathkill Dale (east) 4 3/4 miles

	Grid references	miles
P	SK2196064580	0.00
①	SK2201964545	0.05
②	SK2135463994	0.70
③	SK2074264467	1.30
④	SK2039065130	1.82.
⑤	SK2009465722	2.25
⑥	SK2026666134	2.80
⑦	SK2118065656	3.70
⑧	SK2139165115	4.00

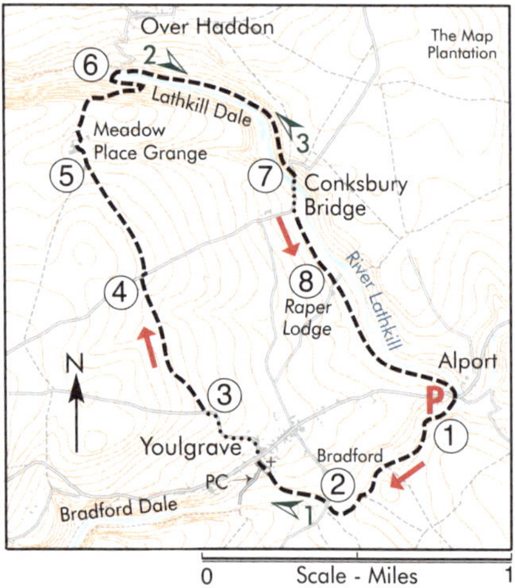

1 Bradford Dale, near Youlgrave

2 comfrey

3 weirs in Lathkill Dale

runs alongside the wall to your right. In about 1/4 mile go over another stile, walking initially alongside a wall. Then you'll see Meadow Place Grange ahead. Bear left downhill and at the wall bear right walking between walls on a muddy track.

5 Go over the (high) stile, next to a gate and follow the wide track, crossing the open farmyard to an entrance between buildings opposite. Walk between the buildings, signed 'Over Haddon.' Go up through a gate and bear slightly right, up the field. In about 200 yards, go through the gate and descend a wide track through woodland. In 1/3 mile you reach a stone slab bridge at Lathkill Dale. The river at this point is often dry, the water running underground to emerge further down the dale.

6 Cross the bridge and turn right at the footpath sign. In May and June you'll see the lovely blue flowers of the comfrey plant, to the right of the path. In about 300 yards there is a short rocky section, followed by a gate. The views along the dale now open out ahead. The river has been tamed by a series of weirs creating pools which provide ideal breeding conditions for brown trout. Look to your right and below is the blue-green, clear deep water of the newly emerged River Lathkill. Known as Blue Waters, the colour may be partly due to dissolved minerals. Follow the path descending down to river level. If you're very lucky you may see a water vole along this stretch of water. Continue along the dale and after about 3/4 mile, you reach a road.

7 Turn right, descending the road to cross the river via Conksbury Bridge. You'll hopefully be able to see brown trout of various sizes, they're unmistakable with their beautiful dappled patterning. Continue along the road, in about 140 yards turn left at a gap in the wall and a footpath sign. Go over another (new) stile and down to a narrow lane.

8 Cross over and through the stile opposite. To the left the riverside fields are managed as flower meadows, a beautiful yellow glory in early summer. Hopefully this view won't be obscured in years to come as a newly planted hedge grows. Continue along the well-defined path as it crosses fields and in about 1/2 mile you reach the road at Alport and the finish. (In 2010 the path was constricted with a fence as it passes the final fields causing it to become muddy, marring the final part of the dale).

Walk 7 ~ Lathkill Dale (west) — 4 3/4 miles

Start: Lay-by, or car park adjacent to a toilet block, half a mile east of Monyash on B5055.
GR: SK15726645. **Map:** OS Exp. OL24.
Distance: 4 3/4 miles (7.6 km). **Allow:** 3 hours.
Terrain: The path along the dale is quite rocky and slippery along the first section. A gentle ascent out of the dale. The narrow grassy path above Lathkill Dale is a little exposed. It is a perfectly safe route but please ensure that children keep to the path and don't stray too close to the dale edge.
Public toilets: At the starting point.
Refreshments: None on the route, but café and pub in nearby Monyash.
Summary of the walk: The walk begins by descending into Lathkill Dale, a beautiful limestone valley, overlooked by crags and interesting rock formations. The dale is noted for its plant life. In June you will see the rare Jacob's Ladder in flower. Leaving the dale, the route winds along an old packhorse track, up a secluded side valley to Haddon Grove. The final section follows an 'open access' path above the dale, giving excellent views. It then passes by the disused Ricklow Quarry, and goes along part of Ricklow Dale before descending back into Lathkill Dale. The final part of the walk retraces outward steps along the head of the dale.
Maximum height: 918ft (280m). **Ascent:** 377ft (115m).

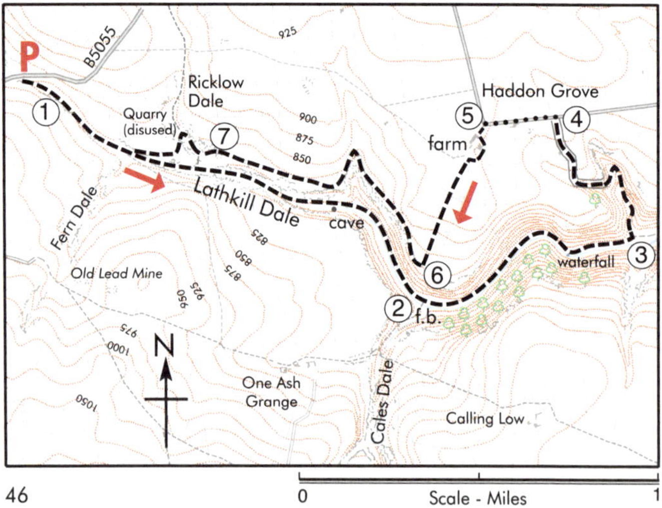

Go through the gate (on the same side of the road as the toilets). Go straight on, along the broad dale. In about 250 yards, there is a dew pond on the right, over the wall. These were used to collect water for cattle. They are now valuable habitats for aquatic life, especially newts.

1 In another 50 yards go through a gate and in about 300 yards through another gate. Then ignore the gate and stile to the right and go through the gate ahead. In about 250 yards there are rocks strewn up the left-hand side of the dale. This is the spoil of the disused Ricklow Marble Quarry. About 350 million years ago, the area was beneath a shallow warm sea. The limestone rock in which shell-like fossils are often found, is itself formed by sea creatures. These were mainly crinoids, a starfish-like animal that lived in the warm seas. As they died in vast numbers over millions of years, the calcium carbonate in their bodies gradually laid down beds of coral, which now form the carboniferous deposits of the Peak District. From here the path becomes rocky, and sometimes slippery underfoot. The rock faces of the dale close in, you pass more rocky spoil and then reach a squeeze stile. Ahead the dale opens out, limestone crags and grassy ledges stretching ahead. Continue straight on, along the stony path. In June you will see the beautiful dark blue flowers of the jacob's ladder plant. Nationally rare, it thrives here. The dale is also an important habitat for orchids, cowslips and many other flowers uncommon elsewhere. In about 1/3 mile there is a cave, Lathkill Head Cave, to your right. This is the source of the River Lathkill, but it is often dry, the water running between the cracks in the limestone bed.

2 In about 1/3 mile there is a footbridge to your right. Keep straight on. By this stage the river should have surfaced, unless there has been a period of dry weather. Amongst the birds to look out for are dippers. This dark brown, white chested bird has a habit of walking underwater, battling against the current, looking for water insects. You may see one on a rock at the edge of the river, doing its characteristic bobbing motion. Then after about 1/3 mile go through a gate and in 250 yards, over a stile. In about 100 yards on the right, is a charming waterfall. In another 280 yards the river is dammed, forming a shallow mill pond. This was the site of Carter's Mill, a corn mill dating to the 18th century.

Walk 7 ~ Lathkill Dale (west) 4 3/4 miles

	Grid references	miles
P	SK1572566452	0.00
①	SK1595766284	0.17
②	SK1745465517	1.35
③	SK1838665758	2.05
④	SK1803866287	2.60
⑤	SK1773266250	2.79
⑥	SK1744265677	3.20
⑦	SK1658966106	4.00

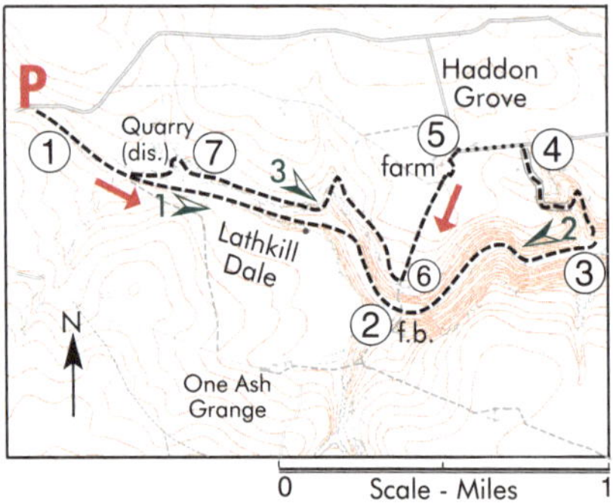

< 1 upper part of Lathkill Dale

< 2 waterfall, Lathkill Dale

< 3 above Lathkill Dale

25 yards further on there is a gate at a wall. Do not go through the gate.

③ Turn left, following the path up alongside the wall. The path widens and goes up the dale. The track was made to be used by packhorse teams bringing supplies to and from the riverside mill, and to the now disused lead mines further along the dale. In 1/4 mile it bends gracefully left and then right as it follows the contours, ensuring the easiest gradients. You go through two gates, past another dew pond and the path levels out. In about 150 yards go over a stile and past Mill Farm and a caravan site to your left. Keep straight on to reach a road junction.

④ Turn left along the quiet road. In 330 yards there is a right-hand bend.

⑤ Turn left at the bend, along the drive of Haddon Grove Farm, signed 'public footpath.' At the end of the drive, just after the farmhouse, you reach a building with a Lathkill Dale information board on the wall.* Turn left here, with the building to your right. On entering the camping field continue along the road until you reach a slanting crossroads. Turn right here and in about 100 yards go through a gateway. Keep straight on for about 50 yards, then look for a stone stile in the left-hand boundary. Turn left over the field and go through the stile. Go straight on, parallel to a wall and descend the field, going through a series of five stiles. When the wall ends, keep straight on down the field towards a gate, and the edge of Lathkill Dale. There are excellent views from now on.

⑥ Go through the gate and turn right to follow a narrow path high above the dale. In about 100 yards the path splits. Ensure you take the right-hand fork, going higher and near to a wall. In 3/4 mile you reach a stile.

⑦ Go over and walk straight on. In about 120 yards there is an area of big boulders at the old quarry. Keep straight on at the (ground level) footpath sign and in 40 yards go through a substantial stone stile. In about 50 yards there's a gate on the left (ignore the larger gate ahead). Turn left here going up rocky steps, in 20 yards bending left uphill. Keep straight on uphill, signed on the right and again over the brow of the hill. The path then slants right, descending to follow a wire fence back into Lathkill Dale. Keep straight on up the dale, retracing outward steps for 1/3 mile to the finish. *By the time you use this book there may be new path signage at the farm. If so, please follow the signs.

Walk 8 ~ Bakewell and the Monsal Trail 3 3/4 miles

Start: Bakewell Agricultural Business Centre, pay-and-display car park. (Closed Mondays).
GR: SK22096874. **Map:** OS Exp. OL24.
Distance: 3 3/4 miles (6.0 km). **Allow:** 2 1/2 hours.
Terrain: Occasionally muddy paths, but mainly surfaced tracks and pavements in Bakewell. One uphill section between points 3 and 4.
Public toilets: At the car park.
Refreshments: Pubs and Cafés in Bakewell. Café at Hassop Station.
Summary of the Walk: The route runs alongside the River Wye out of Bakewell, before gaining height along a walled track. It then descends to the Monsal Trail, a former railway line which leads back to Bakewell.
Maximum height: 689ft (210m). **Ascent:** 288ft (88m).

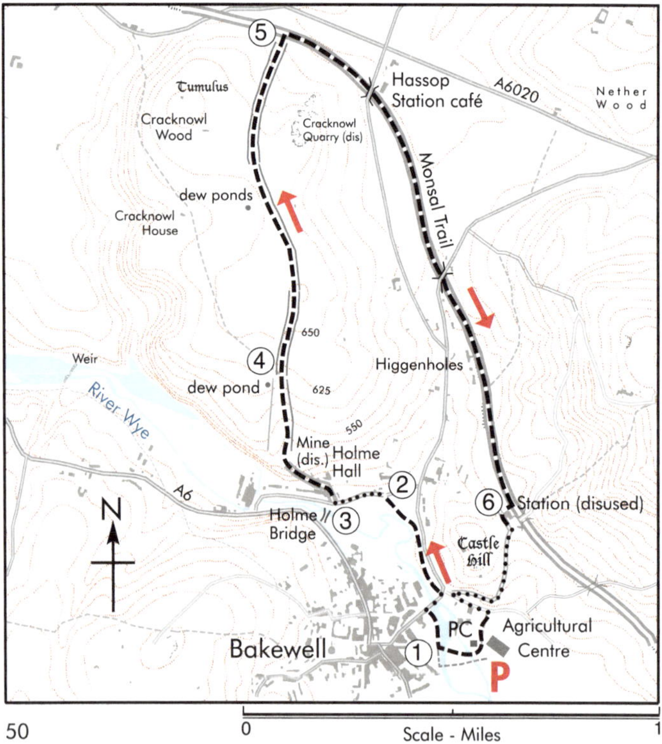

Bakewell dates back to Saxon times, and probably earlier as the springs and the river attracted Iron-Age settlers. The name is from the Anglo-Saxon; 'Baecanwyllan' or maybe 'Baddecanwell,' (Badeca's Springs).

Bakewell Pudding: With a name like Bakewell it was inevitable that a pudding or some such like would be named after it, and so came into being the famous Bakewell Pudding. It is supposed to have been created by accident in about 1860 at the White Horse Inn (now the Rutland Arms). An inexperienced cook was told to make jam tarts. Instead of stirring the eggs and almond mixture into the pastry, she spread jam over the unsweetened pastry and put the mixture on top. When baked it set a little like an egg custard over the plain pastry and was a success. However the story may be just that, as similar puddings were made even in the 16th century. The main difference between a Bakewell Pudding and a Bakewell Tart is that the pudding uses a flaky pastry base and an almond mixture containing eggs. A tart uses a shortcrust pastry base and almond filling, with or without eggs. The tart may also be topped by flaked almonds or icing. There are three shops in Bakewell all selling what they consider to be the best puddings and tarts. Take your pick.

The parking area is large. Part of it is on a field, and part is beyond and to the sides of the agricultural buildings. Wherever you park, walk to the public toilets at the top left corner. This is where the walk starts.

Go over (Mill Leat) footbridge. In 120 yards cross a second footbridge.

(1) After the bridge turn right, alongside the River Wye. You'll see swans and mallards, but look carefully into the clear waters and you should also see brown trout and rainbow trout, both beautifully marked and graceful. At the elegant five-arched bridge the path bends left to the road. Cross over with care (if busy, it may be easier to use the pedestrian reservation to the left). Then turn right, walking over the bridge. Just after the bridge turn left through a metal gate, signed 'Scot's Garden.' This isn't a garden but the riverside meadow. In about 250 yards go through a gate and along the riverside path. In about 100 yards as the river bends left, keep straight on walking to a gate in the wall ahead.

(2) Turn left along the lane for about 200 yards until level with a packhorse bridge on your left. This is Holme Bridge, also known as Sheepwash

Walk 8 ~ Bakewell and the Monsal Trail 3 3/4 miles

	Grid reference	miles
P	SK2209668472 (toilet block, car park)	0.00
①	SK2198668500	0.08
②	SK2175869055	0.65
③	SK2156869025	0.77
④	SK2136769487	1.17
⑤	SK2138870768	2.03
⑥	SK2227169008	3.35

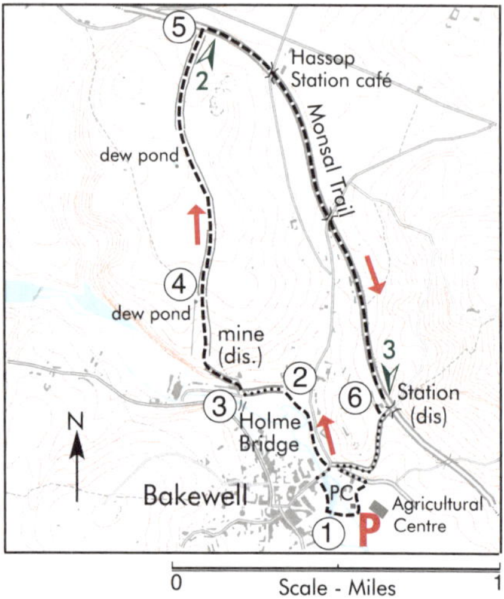

River Wye and Bakewell Bridge

2 Monsal Trail

3 old station, Bakewell

Bridge. It dates from 1664 and enabled packhorse teams to avoid paying the toll on the town centre bridge. The sides (parapets) are low to give clearance to the panniers strapped to the horses.

③ Turn right up the lane opposite, signed as a bridleway. After the housing bear left slightly following the wide uphill track (not the drive parallel with the hall to the right). The lane becomes stony and rises fairly steeply passing to the left of some old mine buildings. This was Holme Bank Chert Mine. Chert is a hard, flinty white rock. It was extracted in large blocks, and brought to the surface on rails. It was mainly made into grindstones which were used to grind flint for the pottery industry. Josiah Wedgwood found that flint ground with chert gave a much whiter body to his wares, than flint ground with gritstones. The mine closed in 1960. In about 130 yards you reach a gate. Go through and follow the tractor track up the field. In 300 yards continue straight on at a marker post, as the track bears left. In about 120 yards ignore the gate to the left. Go straight on to the gate ahead, just beyond a dew pond. Dew ponds are shallow saucer-shaped ponds, collecting and storing water for livestock.

④ Go through the gate, along the walled path signed 'Monsal Trail, Hassop.' Keep straight going through several gates and in 3/4 mile you descend to a junction with a wide track. This is the former trackbed of the Midland Railway line which ran from London to Manchester.

⑤ Turn right along the wide track. In 1/4 mile the track goes under a bridge. (The old Hassop Station is 20 yards beyond). In about 220 yards on the left are picnic tables. Continuing on, you pass beneath another bridge in just under 1/3 mile. After a further 1/2 mile there is an elegant building to the right. This is the former Bakewell station.

⑥ Turn right at the near corner of the building, signed 'Bakewell Station car park.' Cross the car park to the exit, and turn left along the pavement. Ignore roads to either side, keep to the main road as it bends right and goes downhill. In 1/3 mile you reach a slanting junction. Turn sharp left, signed 'town centre' along Coombs Road. Cross over and in 100 yards ignore Rutland Mews to the right. In another 100 yards turn right, signed 'town centre.' Go through a gate to follow the path back into the agricultural centre car park. Now find your car.

Walk 9 ~ Chatsworth Park and Edensor 4 1/4 miles

Start: Calton Lees car park. Fee payable.
GR: SK25876849. **Map:** OS Exp. OL24.
Distance: 4 1/4 miles (6.8 km). **Allow:** 2 1/2 hours.
Terrain: Surfaced tracks, pasture, riverside paths.
Public toilets: None.
Refreshments: Café at Chatsworth Garden Centre near the start. Café at Edensor. (At the Post Office, near the church).
Summary of the Walk: A gentle walk giving great views of Chatsworth Park. From Calton Lees the route begins along an estate lane, gaining height to pass the hamlet of Calton Houses. It then descends parkland giving glorious views on the way to Edensor village. Here, every house is individually designed in a Swiss, Italian or Gothic style. The final section follows the River Derwent with views across to Chatsworth House.
Maximum height: 755ft (230m). **Ascent:** 394ft (120m).

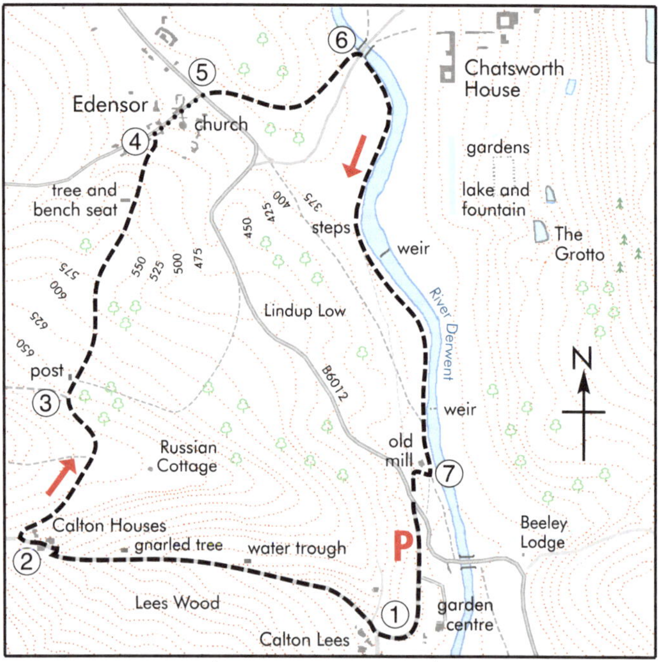

Directions ~ Chatsworth Park and Edensor

Leave the Calton Lees car park and turn right alongside the estate road (away from the main road). Ignore the road to the left (which goes to the garden centre). Keep straight on and in about 300 yards, in Calton Lees village, ignore a road to the left (signed Rowsley).

① Go straight on at the bridleway sign, along a gravel road. In 1/2 mile look out for a water trough on the right. In another 250 yards you pass a venerable gnarled alder tree. After about 300 yards the road bends right, uphill and then left to Calton Houses. After passing the last cottage on the right, continue uphill for about 70 yards to a gate.

② Go through a gate, ignore the path left and walk straight on signed' bridleway' alongside a wall. After about 380 yards, at a path crossroads in the field, go straight on, signed 'Edensor, Chatsworth.' Russian Cottage to the right, was a gift to the 6th Duke of Devonshire from Tsar Nicholas I.

③ Go through a gate after about 90 yards. A walled track leads downhill. At the end of the track go through another gate on to open pasture, with views over Chatsworth Park. (Bench seats here). Turn right going downhill to a guide post (in about 200 yards). Keep straight on ignoring a bridleway to the right, following a path through trees. The path descends to a hollow, with a wood to the right. Keep straight on at the end of the wood heading for a church spire. In 160 yards as the narrow path veers right, keep straight on still towards the spire. In 200 yards there is a single tree with a bench seat on your left. Go past this and keep straight on. You'll soon see a guide post, at which you bear right towards steps and an iron gate. (To the right of a sub-station). If you miss the tree and post don't worry. Head just to the left of the spire, then keep the churchyard fence to your right. At the corner the steps are just to the left.

④ Go up the steps and through the gate, and then down a steep flight of steps to the road. Turn right through the beautiful village of Edensor. (pronounced 'Enzer'). It is a 'model village' having buildings of many styles including Swiss, Italian, Norman and Gothic. It was planned by the architect Joseph Paxton, at the request of the 6th Duke. He was inspired by designs in the 'Encyclopaedia of Cottage, Farm and Villa Architecture,' by John Claudius Loudon,1839. Part of the original village had already been demolished in the 1760s to create open parkland

Walk 9 ~ Chatsworth Park and Edensor $4^{1}/_{4}$ miles

	Grid references	miles
P	SK2587568497	0.00
①	SK2572368443	0.21
	SK2570668443 trough	0.68
②	SK2444468511	1.18
③	SK2473368791	1.44
④	SK2495569836	2.24
⑤	SK2512570013	2.43
⑥	SK2569370157	2.85
⑦	SK2593368760	3.91

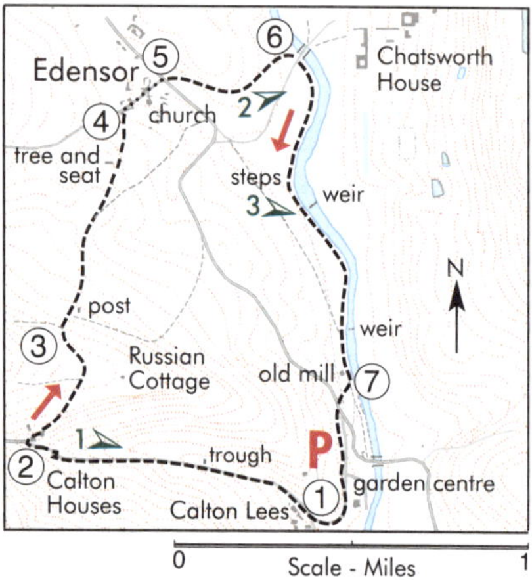

1 on the track to Calton Houses

2 Chatsworth House

3 River Derwent, Chatsworth Park

under Lancelot 'Capability' Brown's instruction. The remainder was removed in the 1830s. The new village was built to the west of what was then a new turnpike road. The church of St Peter's was already on this site. It dates to the 14th century but was greatly enlarged in 1868. Kathleen Kennedy, sister of the late US President, John F. Kennedy is buried here. (She married William Cavendish, the eldest son of the 10th Duke, who was killed in World War II four months later). At the village green, walk along the road to the wrought iron gates and cattle grid.

⑤ Go through the rotating gate and cross the road (take care). The lone house to the right is the only building of the old village not to be moved. The tenant was too old or ill to be disturbed. Follow the wide, surfaced path, running diagonally right through Chatsworth Park. In 1/3 mile the path comes to the estate road, just before the bridge. This elegant three-arched span across the River Derwent was built in the 1760s and designed by James Paine. It gives a lovely view of the river and House.

⑥ Cross the road, and walk beside the river. In just under 1/2 mile, you go up a few steps. You then pass a weir. This is a sort of dam, designed to deepen a river. This one was made in the 1760s by 'Capability' Brown to raise the river so that it could be seen from the House. Continue on the path by the river. On the opposite side of the river you may be lucky to see some of Chatsworth's deer. There are two species in the park; fallow deer, delicate pale brown dappled with white spots and the larger red deer. Ignore any paths that leave the river. In about 1/3 mile, you come to another weir. The ruins 250 yards ahead are the remains of Paine's Mill. It was used for corn grinding. Continue on towards the old mill. The deeper water above the weir was channelled off and controlled along a run, known as a mill race. This current was strong enough to turn a waterwheel, which in turn gave power to the mill. The remains of the old wheel can be seen on the right hand side of the building. The mill was badly damaged by a falling beech tree, in a storm in 1962.

⑦ About 25 yards past the corner of the mill turn sharp right. Follow a path steeply uphill to reach the road. (Ignore the wide grassy diagonally left slanting path). Cross the busy road near the cattle grid and turn left through the gate, back into Calton Lees car park.

Walk 10 ~ Hunting Tower, Chatsworth Park 3 3/4 miles

Start: Chatsworth House car park. Closed 23rd Dec. Opens 9th Jan. Fee payable. For up to date information, visit - www.chatsworth.org.
GR: SK26197034. **Map:** OS Exp. OL24.
Distance: 3 3/4 miles (6.0 km). **Allow:** 2 hours.
Terrain: Mainly well-maintained paths. The steps descending from the Hunting Tower can be slippery after rain or if covered in wet leaves.
Public toilets: Adjacent to the car park.
Refreshments: Café and restaurant at the Stables Courtyard.
Summary of the Walk: Leaving the main car park at Chatsworth House the route takes you through Stand Wood, up past the Aqueduct and on to Swiss Lake. Then alongside Emperor Lake and to the highlight of the walk, the Hunting Tower. This is an Elizabethan gem, built by Bess of Hardwick in about 1582 and barely altered since. It stands at a viewpoint with expansive views over the estate below and far beyond. The final section of the route descends a stepped path back to the parkland parking area.
Maximum height: 853ft (260m). **Ascent:** 426ft (130m).

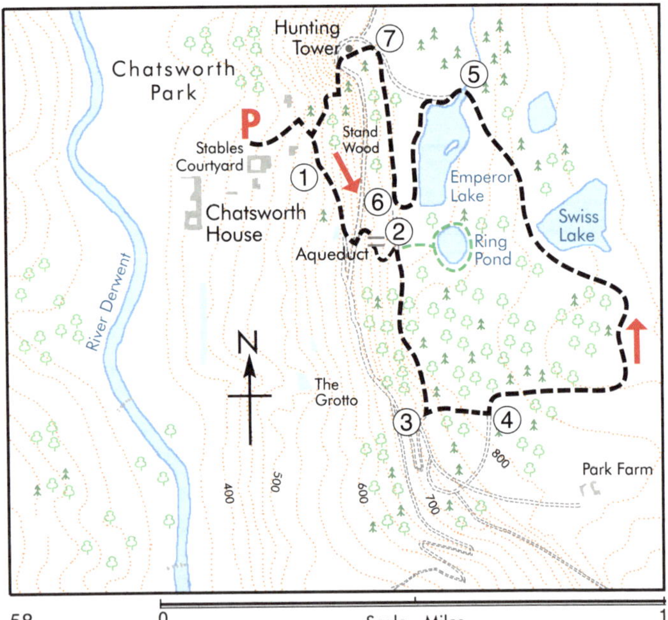

Directions ~ Hunting Tower, Chatsworth Park Walk 10

From the large parking area - walk upwards with the House to your right. At the top right-hand corner, go straight on at a sign 'Farmyard and Playground.' Go through the gateway. (The opening times on the sign apply to the Farmyard. There is unrestricted access to Stand Wood). In 70 yards turn right through a gate giving access to Stand Wood. The road goes up and bends right.

① In about 250 yards bear left at a sign 'The Dell.' In 120 yards, keep straight on at the slanting path crossroads. When you reach a road, cross over to the path opposite. Follow this as it leads beneath an arch of the Aqueduct. It then bends left going uphill. When you're level with the top of the Aqueduct, ignore the steps and turn right. The path then bends left. Ahead is a boulder over which pours the waterfall. This is the Sowter Stone. It has been used to great advantage channelling water to the Aqueduct below. Walk up the rocky steps to the top of the boulder, then turn right for 10 yards to reach a wide track.

② Here there is an optional diversion to see the Ring Pond. To go there cross over and follow the path through woods. In about 200 yards you reach the Ring Pond. This was dug in the 1820s as a reservoir to feed the Aqueduct below. Walk around the pond, in whichever direction you wish and then retrace steps to the wide track. (At point 2).

If you don't want to go to the Ring Pond turn right on the wide track. If you have already been there, turn left on your return to the track. All this area was treeless until the 18th century. Trees were planted and paths laid out in the 1760s by Capability Brown as part of the 4th Duke of Devonshire's Pleasure Gardens. Further work was carried out by Joseph Paxton between 1835 and 1845 for the 6th Duke, when the Aqueduct was constructed and more pathways made. In about 1/3 mile the track descends. Where it levels off look out for a path to the left. (If you reach a tarmac road you've missed it).

③ Turn left here, up through woodland. In 230 yards is a wide gravel track.

④ Turn left here. In just over 1/2 mile you pass to the left of Swiss Lake. It was dug in the 1690s for the 1st Duke, to provide water for the garden cascade. It was simply called the Reservoir until 1839 when the 6th Duke returned from a tour of Europe, enamoured with everything Swiss.

Walk 10 ~ Hunting Tower, Chatsworth Park 3 3/4 miles

	Grid references	miles
P	SK2619470347	0.00
①	SK2646270221	0.30
②	SK2665070079	0.53
③	SK2675669491	1.36
④	SK2694869478	1.49
⑤	SK2688070520	2.50
⑥	SK2665370126	2.83
⑦	SK2659970605	3.25
	SK2650270622 (Hunting Tower)	

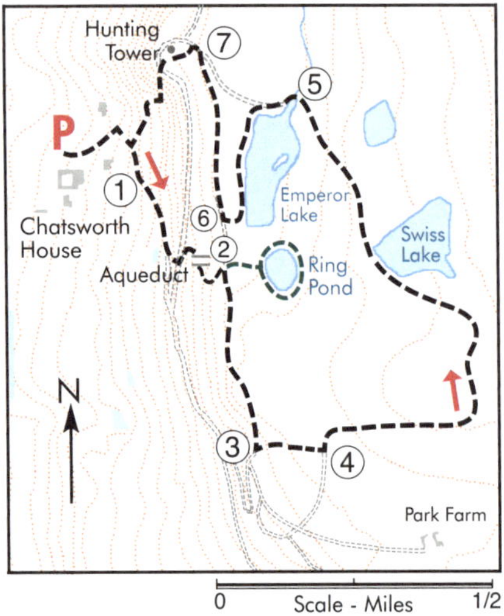

frozen waterfall, Aqueduct

Sowter Stone, above the Aqueduct

Swiss Lake and Swiss Cottage

Continue on the track and in just over 1/3 mile you'll see another lake to your left, Emperor Lake. This is yet another of the glorious 6th Duke's innovations. He had visited Russia and seen the cascades and fountains at Peterhof Palace. He wanted to create a higher gravity-fed fountain to impress Tsar Nicholas I on his proposed visit in 1844. Joseph Paxton was employed to plan and oversee the work. It was a huge undertaking in those days as all the earth had to be removed by shovel and wheel-barrow. The pipe which feeds the fountain, about 380 feet below, is half a mile long and 15 inches wide. The lake and fountain were finished in time for the Tsar's visit. Unfortunately he wasn't able to travel to England and never saw the marvellous Emperor Fountain, named in his honour. The jet is about 260 feet high. It has been recorded at 296 feet and is still the highest gravity-fed fountain in the world.

(5) The path crosses a stream at a narrow inlet. About 30 yards after this, turn left on a path which goes around the right-hand side of the lake. In about 1/4 mile at the far end of the lake there is an overflow structure in the lake (topped with a little spherical iron filter). About 15 yards after this turn right on a path. You reach a path junction in 70 yards.

(6) Turn right along the track and in about 1/4 mile you reach a junction with a tarmac track. Turn left and in about 50 yards there is a wide grassy path at a telegraph pole to your left.

(7) Turn left here and in about 100 yards you come to the Hunting Tower. Walk past with the Tower to your right, to the grassy area in front. This remarkable structure was built on the instruction of Bess (of Hardwick fame) in the 1580s. It was originally called Stand Tower (a stand being a viewpoint). Bess and her attendants would watch the hounds at hunt, from the upper floors. The view from here is far-reaching over Chatsworth Park and beyond. The two cannons 'guarding' the Tower are from a ship that fought at the Battle of Trafalgar. With your back to the Tower walk straight on and down steps to a road. Cross over and walk along the path opposite. A series of steps (can be slippery) take you down the hillside alongside a stream. At the bottom cross the wide track to a path opposite and walk straight on. In about 100 yards you reach a road. Turn right and retrace outward steps for 300 yards to the finish.

Walk 11 ~ Magpie Mine

4 1/4 miles

Start: Free car park, Ashford-in-the-Water.
GR: SK19446976.
Map: OS Exp. OL24.
Distance: 4 1/4 miles (7.2 km).
Allow: 2 1/2 hours.
Terrain: Field paths, quiet lanes, farm tracks, woodland and riverside paths. One main ascent at the start of the walk. The riverside path in particular can be very muddy.
Public toilets: At the car park.
Refreshments: Pubs in Ashford-in-the-Water and Sheldon (off-route).
Summary of the Walk: Starting at the beautiful village of Ashford-in-the-Water the route quickly gains height, giving great views along the River Wye valley and beyond. After a short section on quiet lanes the highlight of the walk, the remains of Magpie Mine come into view. These are probably the best preserved remains of any British lead mine. The mine dates from the 1740s and was eventually closed in 1958. From there the route crosses fields to reach the eastern edge of Sheldon village, before descending an attractive wooded valley. The final section follows the meandering River Wye, back towards Ashford-in-the-Water.
Maximum height: 1066ft (325m). **Ascent:** 656ft (200m).

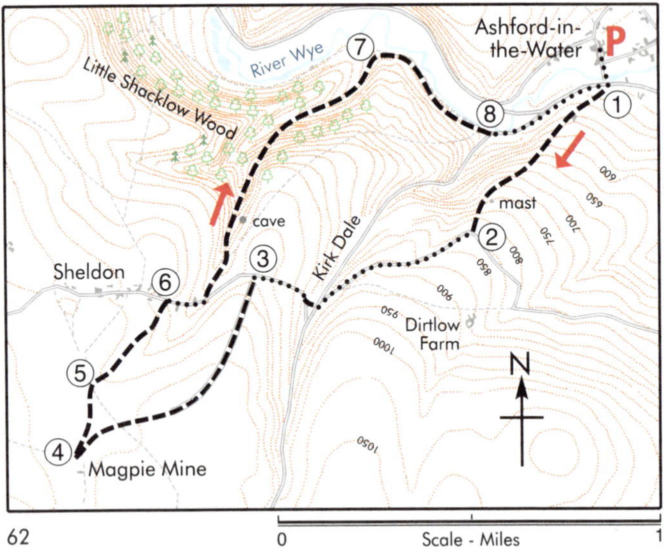

Directions ~ Magpie Mine Walk 11

From the car park, walk back to the road junction. Turn left along Fennel Street. Where the road bends sharp left, continue straight on passing to the right of the open-sided hexagonal structure. This was constructed to mark the Queen's Silver Jubilee in 1977. Keep straight on to a bridge, over the River Wye. This is Sheepwash Bridge, as the name suggests sheep were once washed in the river before being sheared. Originally this was a medieval packhorse bridge, but over the years has been altered and widened. Prior to there being a bridge, there was a ford, enabling packhorses to cross the river as they followed the Roman, Portway trading route. The village grew up to take advantage of this. Cross the bridge. You may see brown trout in the fast-flowing water. Cross the main road with care to the pavement and footpath sign.

① At the sign, go through a gate and follow a tarmac track uphill. After passing a house in about 200 yards, the route is on grass. Walk straight on, the path passing to the right of three large trees. It then wends up towards the mast. After the mast, walk slightly to the left towards a gate in the wall and a footpath sign.

② Go through the gate and turn right along the road, in just under 1/2 mile you come to a road junction. Cross the road and go over the stile opposite and up the field to a gate. Turn right on the road for about 230 yards, to a track on the left.

③ Turn left along the signed, walled track as it ascends gradually to open fields. In 1/3 mile the track ends at a gate and a stile. Go over the step stile onto the open field. The path is initially indistinct, but walk straight on towards a footpath post at a broken wall. Then walk straight on to the next footpath post at a path crossroads. Keep straight on again, heading towards the Magpie Mine buildings. In about 80 yards go through a small gate and immediately over a step-stile, and head for the mine buildings. Take a while to explore around and then return to the main round chimney. Magpie Mine was a lead mine, it opened in the 1740s and was closed and reopened numerous times right up until 1958. It never made much money for successive owners and shareholders and very often investors made substantial losses. This was partly because the main shaft was very deep at 729 feet and flooded con-

Walk 11 ~ Magpie Mine

4 1/4 miles

	Grid references	miles
P	SK1944369767	0.00
①	SK1944869581	0.18
②	SK1886569021	0.71
③	SK1798768854	1.34
④	SK1726968189	2.04
⑤	SK1731768429	2.20
⑥	SK1777468783	2.50
cave	SK1793969178	2.88
⑦	SK1849569721	3.42
⑧	SK1895769413	3.75

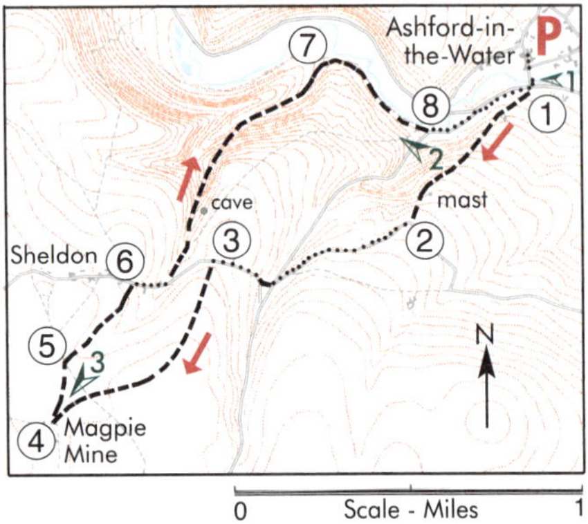

1 Sheepwash Bridge, Ashford-in-the-Water

2 River Wye and the A6

3 Magpie Mine

stantly. In the 1840s a Cornish beam engine replaced an earlier Newcomen Engine to pump water to the surface. This was coal fired and expensive to operate. Therefore a sough (basically a long drain) was blasted and bored from the bottom of the shaft, draining water to the Rive Wye, near Ashford just over a mile away. This took eight years to complete owing to very hard rock and other problems, and was finished in 1881. By that time lead prices had fallen, making the mine uneconomic. It was then operated spasmodically, with little success until 1958. Read the little notice behind the round chimney, telling of a dark deed.

(4) With your back to the round chimney, turn to face the way you came into the mine area (a little round building is a marker). You'll then see a wall just to your left (about 30 degrees to the left of the path you came in on) Follow the path running along the right-hand side of the wall. You'll soon reach a step stile at the wall corner and a tree. Go over the stile and walk straight on across the field.

(5) At the next stile, go over and turn right at the sign 'Ashford'. During the next 350 yards you'll go over three step-stiles as you cross the many limestone walls criss-crossing this area. The fourth step-stile is a wooden one over a fence. You then walk a few yards and go through a gap-stile and follow a farm track down to the road.

(6) Turn right here, and in 160 yards, after passing a house on the right is gate and a footpath sign. Turn left here descending the valley. In about 100 yards the path divides. Take the path bearing left, descending into a wooded valley. A gate leads into the attractive beech wood valley. Look out for a cave entrance on the right (do not enter) and some overgrown mining remains alongside the path. In just over 1/2 mile you go through a gate to leave the wooded area. Follow the path alongside a wall, descending down to the main path along the River Wye.

(7) At the path junction, turn right, go through a gate and follow the path alongside the River Wye. In 1/3 mile you'll reach a road.

(8) Go through the gate and walk straight on along the road. At the road junction with the main road, turn right along the pavement, and cross with care when safe. Then turn left, walking back over Sheepwash Bridge and retracing your steps to the car park.

Walk 12 ~ Ashford and Headstone Tunnel 4 miles

Start: Car park, off Fennel Street, Ashford-in-the-Water. Free. **GR:**SK19446976. Or park at the lay-by, near Sheepwash Bridge.
Map: OS Exp. OL24.
Distance: 4 miles (6.4 km). **Allow:** 2 hours.
Terrain: Field paths, walled track, a section of the Monsal Trail.
Public toilets: At the car park and at Monsal Head.
Refreshments: Pub and Café in Ashford. Pub and café at Monsal Head.
Summary of the Walk: Starting from the attractive village of Ashford-in-the-Water. The route gains height gradually to reach Monsal Head, a view-point over the beautiful Monsal Dale. The route descends quite steeply to the viaduct, then takes you through the newly re-opened Headstone Tunnel, 533 yards long. The Monsal Trail is popular with cyclists especially now the tunnels are open. It is wide enough for everyone, but you do need to be aware. Field paths lead back down to Ashford-in-the-Water and the finish. A few step-stiles.
Maximum height: 886ft (270m). **Ascent:** 525ft (160m).

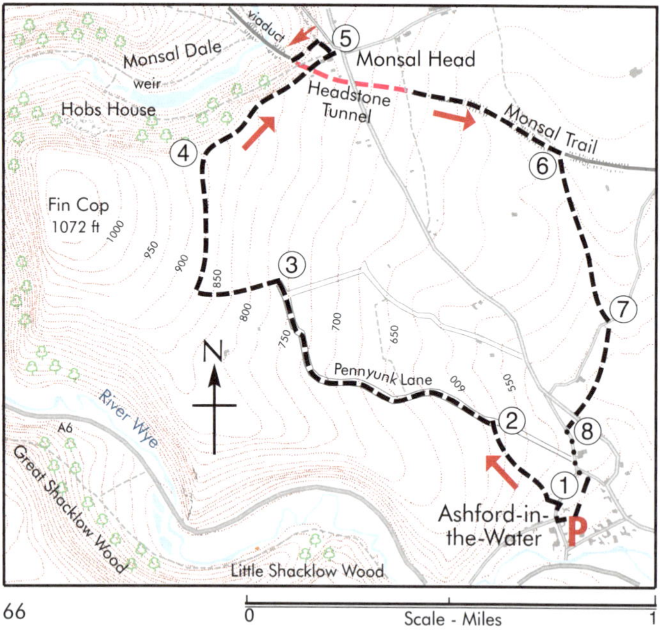

Directions ~ Ashford and Headstone Tunnel Walk 12

From the car park, walk back to the road junction. Cross over and turn right up Vicarage Lane. Note the sculpture of a man's head positioned on a house wall. Walk up the road for about 70 yards.

(1) Turn sharp left up the path at a footpath sign. It goes up by the side of a fence to a stile at a field boundary. Go through the stile and bear slightly right across the field, passing a marker guide post, then in the same direction to reach a stile in a wall.

(2) Go over the stile and turn left along a walled track, Pennyunk Lane. After passing a house on your right, look out for the distinctive ridges in one of the fields to the right. This may be the remains of the medieval method whereby people farmed strips of land rather than large fields. The track gains height gradually. In 3/4 mile it bends right, there is a dew pond on the left. This has been restored to attract amphibians such as newts. The stone built, saucer shaped bowls were lined with clay and used to collect rain for livestock. (Some, like this were concrete). Stainless steel pipe-fed troughs replaced them long ago. If there are cows in the fields when you walk try to identify the breed. You may see the black and white friesians, brown and white simmental, or a white and bluey grey cow - the belgian blue. Even the stones in the track are of interest. The shiny black smooth ones are black marble, really just black limestone which was quarried near Ashford-in-the-Water. It was popular for table tops in Victorian times. In another 1/4 mile the walled track ends.

(3) Turn left, go through the stile and walk up the field alongside the wall. At the top go through a stile and turn right, signed 'Monsal Dale.' Pass another dew pond to your right, then go through a gate and follow another walled track. Go through three more gates and then reach a sign and two seats (an ideal rest point).

(4) Turn right at the sign 'Monsal Head' following the path running along the edge of the dale. In about 1/3 mile ignore the path sharp left and reach the stile at Monsal Head in about 20 yards. This is a great view-point over Monsal Dale and the surrounding hills. There is a café, pub and public toilets here. The viaduct below, the Headstone Viaduct, once carried trains of the Midland Railway Line which ran from London to Manchester. It opened in 1863 and closed in 1968. It now forms the

Walk 12 ~ Ashford and Headstone Tunnel 4 miles

	Grid references	miles
P	SK1944369767	0.00
①	SK1939369827	0.07
②	SK1913670151	0.34
③	SK1830770677	1.06
④	SK1801671146	1.60
⑤	SK1845371548	1.97
⑥	SK1939871184	2.87
⑦	SK1959770537	3.31
⑧	SK1942670144	3.61

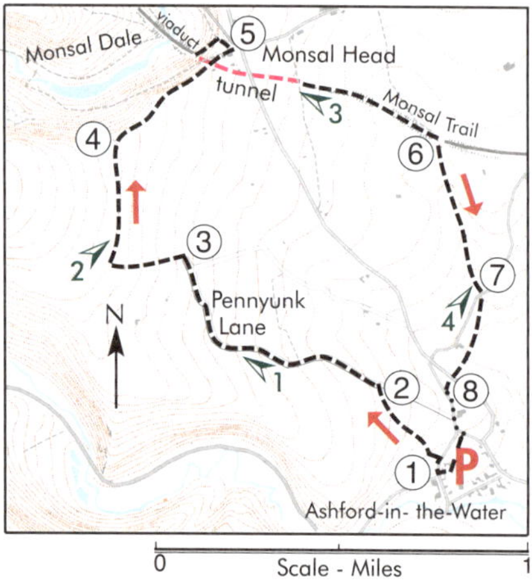

1 Pennyunk Lane

2 dew pond

3 Headstone Tunnel (exit)

4 turning hay

Monsal Trail, an 8 1/2 mile route between Bakewell and Topley Pike junction (3 miles east of Buxton). The previously closed tunnels along its length were re-opened in May 2011. They are lit until dusk every day. The distinctive hill beyond the viaduct on the left side of the dale is Fin Cop. This was the site of an Iron Age fort, constructed around 400BC. It was excavated in 2009/10 and nine skeletons were found.

(5) With your back to the road, turn right at the sign 'Upperdale and Monsal Viaduct.' Descend the stepped, fairly steep path and in about 60 yards, turn left descending a steep path to the Monsal Trail.

Turn left to enter the Headstone Tunnel. It is 533 yards long (1/3 mile). Keep to the left and beware of bikes. The trail can get very busy. Emerging into the light, continue along the trail for nealy half a mile. On the way look out for the wind-up audio guide which gives recordings of railway related history - including the brilliant 'Monsal Trail Blues.'

Just diagonally opposite the sign on the left to 'Little Longstone', look for a sign on the right - 'Ashford.'

(6) Descend the steps of the stile, walk straight on across the field to the next stile. Keep walking straight on alongside a wall, going through another three stiles. Then walk across the corner of a field to a stile at a road.

(7) Go through the stile and cross the road and go through another stile and walk straight on, a wall to your left. In about 180 yards go through a gate and straight on to another gate. Then descend the field to an old barn in the hollow.

Go through the stile to the right of the barn and follow a narrow walled path up to a road.

Cross the road diagonally left and go through a small gate signed 'Ashford.' Cross a field to a stile.

(8) Go through the stile and turn left along the lane and in about 170 yards, bear left down a lane called 'Hill Cross.' Ignore the first footpath sign on the right, and in about 100 yards turn right at the second 'public footpath' sign. The path leads to a children's play area and field. Walk straight on with the wall to your right, passing a cemetery and then through a gap back to the car park. If you have time, Ashford-in-the-Water is a beautiful village to wander around.

Walk 13 ~ Monsal Dale — $3^1/4$ miles

Start: Long-stay car park, Monsal Head. Or roadside parking along the road opposite.
GR: SK18517152. **Map:** OS Exp. OL24.
Distance: 3 1/2 miles (5.6 km). **Allow:** 2 hours.
Terrain: Farm tracks, field paths. Well-worn and sometimes muddy paths along Monsal Dale.
The track (between points 1 and 2) is unfortunately, and legally, used by off-road motorbikes and other vehicles. Sundays are the worst days, so I advise if possible avoiding this route on Sundays.
Public toilets: At the car park.
Refreshments: Café and pub at Monsal Head.
Summary of the Walk: Starting from Monsal Head, one of the most scenic spots in the Peak District, the walk descends to the Monsal Trail at the viaduct. After crossing the viaduct the route leaves the trail, gaining height to give great views down into Monsal Dale and across the surrounding hills. The route then descends a winding track through woodland, back into Monsal Dale. The final section follows the winding River Wye through the dale, reaching a weir. After crossing a bridge here, the final section is uphill back to Monsal Head.
Maximum height: 984ft (300m). **Ascent:** 705ft (215m).

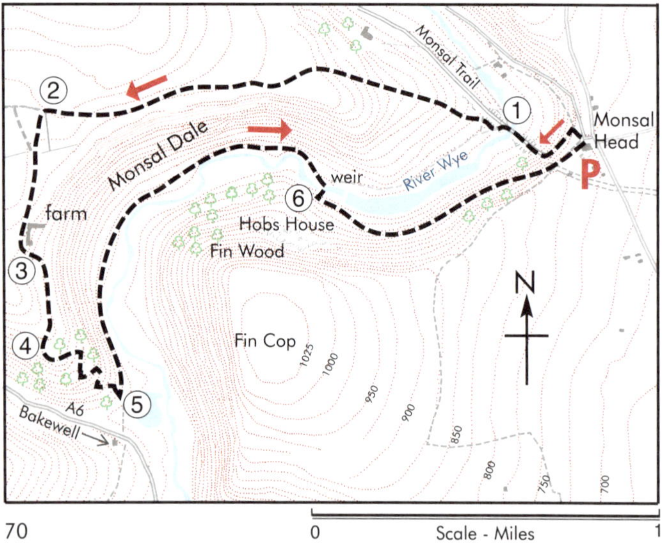

From the car park, walk to the right of the Stables Bar and turn left on the road to the corner. The railway trackbed below and the impressive viaduct were once part of the route between Derby and Buxton, providing a direct link with London. It was built by the Midland Railway Company in 1867 and closed in 1968. The Headstone Viaduct, often called Monsal Viaduct, is now a much-loved part of the landscape. Monsal Head incidentally used to be called Headstones Head. Not everyone was happy when the railway and the viaduct were constructed in the pristine valley. John Ruskin, artist, critic and author, said rather ungraciously; 'the valley is gone and the Gods with it, and now every fool in Buxton can be at Bakewell in half an hour and every fool in Bakewell at Buxton...' The five-arched viaduct is nearly 80 feet high and despite Ruskin's opinion, it is now a preserved and much-loved structure. The trackbed of the disused railway is now part of the Monsal Trail, a walking and cycling route, 8 1/2 miles long between Bakewell and Topley Pike Junction (just to the east of Buxton).

(1) Go through the wide gap in the wall and turn right, signed 'Upperdale and Monsal Viaduct.' Walk down the steps and in 60 yards is a bench and a sign 'Viaduct and Monsal Trail.' Turn left, descending quite steeply to the viaduct. At the bottom turn right, walking along the viaduct. 65 yards after the viaduct turn left at a sign for 'Brushfield.' Go through the gate and continue straight on, walking uphill (ignore path to the left). In 1/4 mile the path joins a wider track. Continuing straight on uphill. Beware of motorbikes and other vehicles along here, especially on Sundays. The stony path winds uphill and levels out after about 300 yards. To the left there is an open area giving great views across and along Monsal Dale. Note the rocky spires on the opposite hillside. This looks like an old quarry, but is a landslip, known as Hobs House. In folklore, Hob was a giant who emerged from his stony home at night to secretly help local farmers. In return they left him food and drink. The hill above is called Fin Cop, once used as the site of an Iron Age fort, constructed about 400BC. It has the remains of bank and ditch fortifications running around the summit. In just under 1/2 mile, you pass through two gates within 170 yards. A few yards after the second

Walk 13 ~ Monsal Dale 3 1/4 miles

	Grid references	miles
P	SK1851071522	0.00
①	SK7809474890	0.07
②	SK1678871652	1.19
③	SK1674271235	1.46
④	SK1679071025	1.60
⑤	SK1704070741	1.87
⑥	SK1764371429	2.74

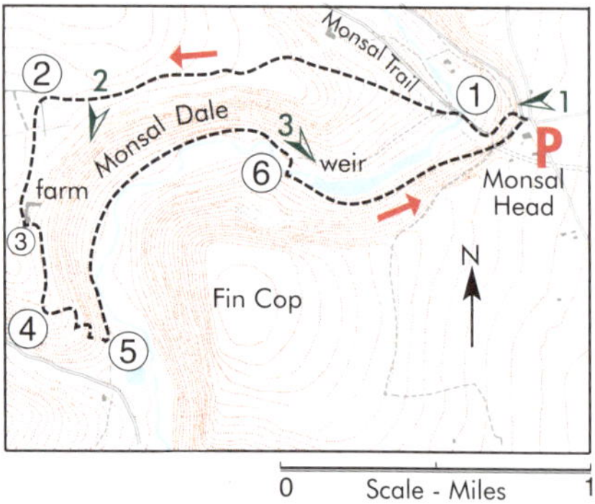

1 Headstone Viaduct and Monsal Dale from Monsal Head

2 simmental cattle

3 weir, Monsal Dale

gate, at the end of the wall is a footpath sign 'Lees Bottom, White Lodge.'

(2) Turn left here walking diagonally right across the field to a gateway and farm track. Go through the gateway, signed 'Brushfield Hough Farm only,' and continue along the farm track. Pass by a modern barn, then an old stone-built barn. Then follow the track as it bends left, (signed with a yellow arrow). Walk downhill for about 20 yards, with an old disused barn to your right. After the building is a gate.

(3) Go through the gate (yellow arrowed) then through another gateway and bear left, joining the prominent track running alongside a wall. After about 200 yards there is a footpath sign and a stile at the wall. You're quite likely to see a buzzard in the Peak District. They are mostly seen soaring high above, looking out for voles and rabbits. They have a wing span of about four feet and often make a slow 'mewing' noise.

(4) Turn left here going over the stile and then bear right, following a path zig-zagging quite steeply through woodland. You may see or hear, amongst other birds, willow warbler, chiffchaff and nuthatch.

In just over 1/3 mile you reach the main path through Monsal Dale.

(5) Turn left at the path junction and follow the wide path as it winds its way through the dale. Along this stretch of the river you may see dippers and grey wagtails, if you're very lucky maybe a kingfisher. In just over 3/4 mile you'll see what looks like a waterfall, but is a man-made weir. I'm not sure, but I think the weir was made in order to aerate the water for the benefit of the trout downstream. The River Wye is a popular fly-fishing river and weirs are often used at other locations for this purpose. It may also have been made to power a mill, but I can't find any specific information about this. Before the weir is a footbridge.

(6) Turn right, over the footbridge. Turn left at the other side, the path taking you alongside the weir. After heavy rain it is an impressive sight as the water thunders and churns, creating a fine spray. Keep well back from the edge. Leaving the weir, continue along the narrow path as it climbs back up towards Monsal Head. In just under 1/2 mile you'll emerge from the tree-lined path, the beautiful dale now visible again. Go through the gap and retrace your steps back to the car park.

Walk 14 ~ Miller's Dale 2 3/4 miles

Start: Roadside parking, Cressbrook Mill.
GR: SK17337267. **Map:** OS Exp.OL24.
Distance: 2 3/4 miles (4.4 km). Main route.
Allow: 1 1/2 hours.
Terrain: Dale paths; can be muddy. Field paths and a section of road walking. The dale can sometimes flood at the Cressbrook end - see directions for the 'flood route' if this is the case. The alternative route using the Monsal Trail is very popular with cyclists, the track is wide but you need to be aware of them. The alternative route is about 1/4 mile longer than the main route.
Public toilets and Refreshments: None, nearest at Monsal Head.
Summary of the Walk: This short route passes the former Cressbrook Mill (now residential) and follows Miller's Dale. The first section of this attractive dale is known as Water-cum-Jolly. There are impressive limestone crags alongside the river. After passing Litton Mill there is a choice - return via the newly opened (May 2011) tunnels on the former railway line, part of the Monsal Trail. The tunnels are lit until dusk and are used by walkers, cyclists and horse-riders. Or for the full route, climb out of the dale for lovely views, then pass the village of Cressbrook. Finally you follow a quiet lane down the hill back to the parking area at the former mill.
Maximum height: 986ft (295m). **Ascent:** 558ft (170m). (Main route).

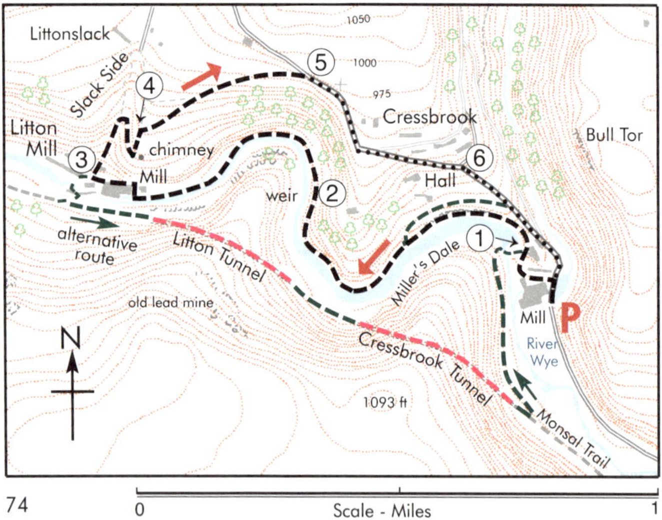

Directions ~ Miller's Dale — Walk 14

From the parking area, look out for the sign 'Concession footpath Litton Mill.' Turn left here walking alongside the former Cressbrook Mill. This elegant Georgian style building was finished in 1815 as an extension of the older mill built in 1787. They were cotton-spinning mills producing yarn (thread) from prepared cotton. The mill was originally powered by a waterwheel, and in the 1890s was converted to water-powered turbines. In the 1800s children as young as seven were forced to work in the mill. Continue on, walking alongside a man-made water run. This is the mill race and would have provided a controllable stream to turn a waterwheel, which gave power to the mill. At the end of this is a footbridge and the start of Miller's Dale, the section here being known as Water-cum-Jolly. Before you go over the footbridge you may wish to walk to your left a few yards for the view of the limestone crag reflected in the mill pond. This is known to climbers as the Rubicon Wall. Although only about 70 feet high it has some very hard routes. Return to the first footbridge. (If the path is flooded refer to the end of the instructions).

(1) Go over the footbridge, passing the sign about this being a concessionary path etc. The path passes beneath the crags and alongside the placid waters of the mill pond. Beyond the pond there are areas which are 'swampy' in appearance but which are good for wildlife. In March you'll see lots of frogs and frogspawn in the shallow water.

(2) In just about 3/4 mile you'll see the remains of a waterwheel near a weir. This was used to pump water up to Cressbrook village in the early 1900s. Along here you may also see brown trout as they dart for insects. About 1/3 mile past the weir you'll pass through a gateway and then the imposing building of the former Litton Mill comes into view. The wide track bears right crossing the former mill race and then left. You pass the former mill buildings that have now been converted into apartments. At the end of the mill area, you pass through a large gateway, the pillars either side surmounted by stone spheres. (If the gates are across, there is a stepped exit about 50 yards before the gateway on the left). There is now an alternative 'tunnel route' back to Cressbrook Mill.

(3) **Alternative** - From the gateway walk straight on and in about 80 yards turn left at a house corner, signed 'Monsal Trail to Miller's Dale.' Cross

Walk 14 ~ Miller's Dale 2 3/4 miles

	Grid references	miles
P	SK1733472679	0.00
①	SK1720972816	0.17
②	SK1661673004	0.96
③	SK1596673006	1.52
④	SK1614273156	1.96
⑤	SK1665173259	2.18
⑥	SK1708173054	2.52

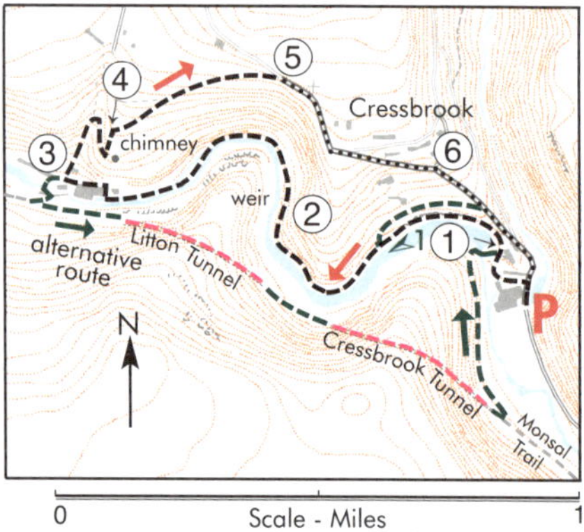

Litton Tunnel (alternative route)

chimney, above Litton Mill

≺1 Miller's Dale ©Keith Daniels

the footbridge and go up the path to the former railway line. Turn left signed 'Bakewell' and in just over 1/4 mile you enter the first tunnel, Litton Tunnel (about 1/4 mile). Then after a short distance in the open you go through Cressbrook Tunnel (about 1/3 mile). After this, in about 100 yards turn sharp left signed 'Cressbrook.' Keep on the narrow path ignoring a minor path to the left in 110 yards. After a further 350 yards the path descends rocky steps to a footbridge. In a few yards you rejoin the outward route, turning right past the mill to the parking area.

(3) **Main route** - Immediately after passing through the gateway, turn sharp right, back on yourself going up a narrow road. Note the distinctively shaped chimneys of the houses. In 130 yards at a left-hand bend keep straight on and up, ignoring the footpath sign to the left. In another 60 yards go through a gate (or over stile) and walk up the valley on a grassy track. In about 100 yards the track forks. Take the right-hand path just before a telegraph pole, and continue ascending the valley side. As you reach the top at a left-hand bend, notice the stubby round chimney in the field to your right. Surprisingly, this is the chimney from the boiler house at Litton Mill, far below. Most of the flue is within the hillside. In 80 yards there is a gate, stile and footpath sign on your right.

(4) Go through the gate (or over stile) and follow the green track as it contours above Miller's Dale giving great views. See if you can pick out Monsal Head. In about 300 yards go through a gate and continue on the walled track. In just under 1/4 mile you reach a road junction.

(5) Turn right going along the road, shortly passing a church. 250 yards after the church continue straight on down the hill, ignoring the road bearing left. In another 300 yards, you pass the entrance to Cressbrook Hall on your right and in a few yards reach another road junction.

(6) Bear right continuing steeply downhill. Halfway down the hill on the left is a conveniently situated, stone memorial seat. At the bottom of the hill you'll be back at the parking area and the finish of the walk.

'Flood route.' Return to the road and turn left. Take the left fork, going uphill. In 180 yards (after the last house) go through a gap in the wall. Follow the path and in 1/3 mile it descends a rocky section to rejoin the dale. Turn right and follow the main route and you'll reach 'point 2.'

Walk 15 ~ Cressbrook Dale 4 1/4 miles

Start: Roadside parking, Cressbrook Mill.
GR: SK17347266. **Map:** OS Exp. OL24.
Distance: 4 1/4 miles (6.8 km). **Allow:** 2 1/2 hours.
Terrain: Dale paths; can be muddy. Field paths and two short sections of quiet lanes. A few step-stiles between points 6 and 8.
Public toilets: None.
Refreshments: Pub in Litton and the post office serves refreshments.
Summary of the Walk: From Cressbrook the route goes uphill on a lane before descending to Ravensdale Cottages. It follows Cressbrook Dale where there is a choice of routes. Climb out of the dale for great views or follow the path along the dale. It then follows Tansley Dale to Litton. Field paths then lead back to the edge of Cressbrook Dale and to the finish.
Maximum height: 968ft (295m). **Ascent:** 804ft (245m).

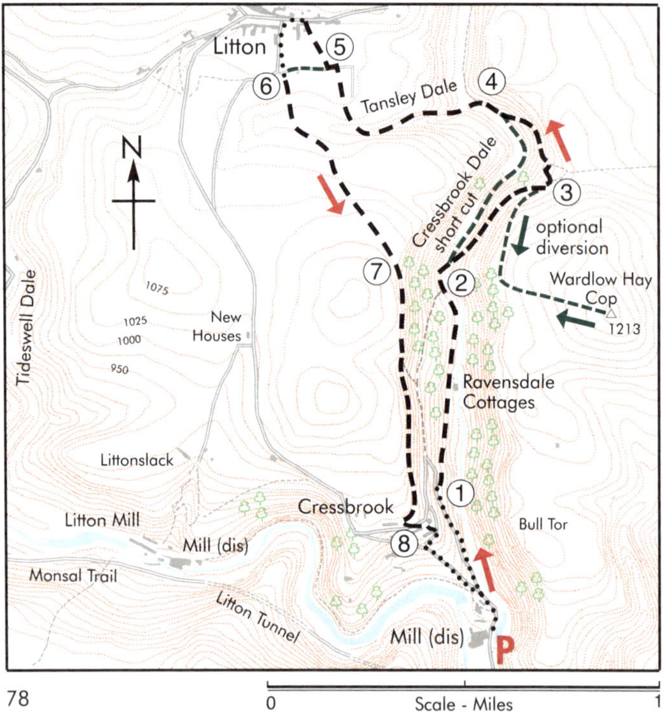

From the lay-by, walk straight on uphill on a road signed 'Cressbrook, Litton.' (Ignore the road to the left).

(1) After 1/2 mile, turn right along a narrow road, signed 'Ravensdale - No Through Road,' walking downhill. In 1/4 mile you pass the secluded Ravensdale Cottages. Keep straight on at the public footpath sign, then go through a gate to follow a path through trees into Cressbrook Dale. In April or May you should see delicate white flowers with spear-shaped dark green leaves. These are ramsons (wild garlic). In 1/4 mile the path narrows, and you cross a footbridge. A sign to the right gives details of the Cressbrook Dale nature reserve. In about 100 yards the path forks. You have a choice here - the full route follows the right-hand path going uphill. Or you can take a short cut, avoiding the hill.

(2) **Short-cut**: Walk straight on, along the left-hand path. Somewhere in Cressbrook Dale on a rock in a stream is one of the world's rarest plants. This is the only known location of the Derbyshire feather moss. The exact position is kept a secret. After the woods the dale opens out, the path following the stream (which often runs dry higher up the dale). Continue on, until you reach some stepping stones. See Point 4.

(2) **Full route**: Take the right-hand path going uphill. There are a couple of rocky sections, but nothing too difficult. In spring look out for the long yellowy catkins of the hazel trees that line the path. A catkin is a cylindrical flower structure without petals, covered with pollen to enable it to be blown to pollinate other trees or carried by insects, particularly bees. In 1/3 mile you leave the trees and the views open up across the dale.

(3) The path levels out and you reach a wall corner. There is an optional diversion here (about 1/2 mile each way) to Wardlow Hay Cop (hill).

Diversion - At the wall corner, turn sharp right and walk with the wall to your left, the dale to your right. In 1/4 mile turn left going through a gate in the wall. Walk uphill along a narrow path to reach the trig. point of Wardlow Hay Cop. At 1,213 feet it is the highest point in the area, with expansive views. Reverse your steps to return to the main route.

(3) At the wall corner bear left slightly, (or go straight on, if returning from the diversion) to follow a path down into the dale. At the bottom bear right. In 160 yards there are stepping stones over the (often dry) stream.

Walk 15 ~ Cressbrook Dale 4 1/4 miles

	Grid references	miles
P	SK1733472679	0.00
①	SK1714073254	0.42
②	SK1718374162	1.03
③	SK1755974492	1.35
	SK1784873982 Wardlow Hay Cop	
④	SK1728774822	1.68
⑤	SK1670574959	1.98
⑥	SK1649274933	2.28
⑦	SK1696274159	2.88
⑧	SK1705473140	3.61

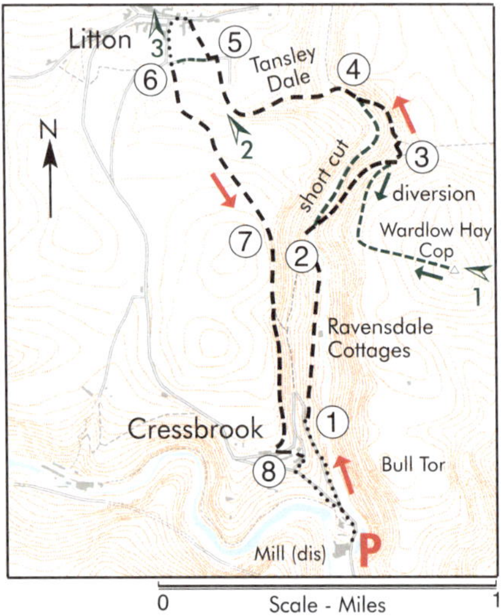

≺3 Red Lion, Litton

≺1 Sandy at Wardlow Hay Cop

≺2 near Litton

④ Turn left, over the stones, through a gate and walk up Tansley Dale. After about 1/3 mile the path bears right, going up alongside a wall to a stile at a wall corner. Go over the stile, bearing right to a wall corner and signpost. Bear right here, walking to a gate and stile.

⑤ Go over the stile, and turn left along the track. (If you don't want to go into Litton continue on the track for about 200 yards and rejoin the main route (at point 6). For Litton, walk 50 yards and go over a stile to the right. Walk diagonally left to the far left-hand corner of the field. Go over the stile and turn left on the road. In about 200 yards there is a road to the left signed 'Cressbrook, Monsal Dale.' After visiting the attractive village, return here and walk along the road for about 250 yards to a junction with a farm track, where the road bends sharp right.

⑥ Turn left on the track for 15 yards and then turn right at a sign, over a stile. Walk straight on down the field and go over the stile in the wall ahead. Then bear left over a field to a stile. Go over the stile and bear right up a field to a stile. Go through the stile, cross a farm track, over the stile and walk up the field to a stile in the left-hand wall. Go over the stile and head for a gate and stile in the top left-hand corner of the field. Go over the stile and walk straight on to a post at the top left-hand field corner. Go through the stile at the footpath sign and walk towards the left-hand wall and a small gate.

⑦ Go through the gate and turn right, following a narrow path above Cressbrook Dale. In 150 yards the path forks but they both rejoin soon after. In about 180 yards, ignore steps descending left. In 330 yards go through a gate, continue straight on, going through another gate in about 400 yards. The path approaches a house. Don't be put off as this is the way - at the house turn left, walking between the house and a shed (the house wall to your right). In a few yards the path bends left, and you walk downhill to a road. You are now in Cressbrook.

⑧ Cross the road and follow the footpath opposite, down the village green, with a Millenium Stone to the right. After about 80 yards you come to another road. Turn right and in 110 yards is another road junction. Turn left descending the hill. Look out for the memorial seat on the left. In another 1/4 mile, you'll be back at the parking area.

Walk 16 ~ Gardom's Edge

3 1/4 miles

Start: Birchen Edge car park (free). Robin Hood. Off the A619, near Baslow.
GR: SK28027214. **Map:** OS Exp. OL24.
Distance: 3 1/4 miles (5.2 km). **Allow:** 2 hours.
Terrain: Grassy paths, some boggy and wet areas after rain. Two step-stiles.
Public toilets: None. **Refreshments:** The Robin Hood Inn, near the start.
Summary of the Walk: The route gains height to reach Gardom's Edge. There is an optional short diversion from Gardom's Edge to see a standing stone. The whole area between Gardom's and Birchen Edges was a Bronze Age settlement. Archaeologists have discovered evidence of wooden roundhouses and agriculture. From Gardom's Edge the route crosses moorland towards Birchen Edge. The final part of the walk descends back to Robin Hood. Keep children a safe distance away from rock edges.
Maximum height: 984ft (300m). **Ascent:** 295ft (90m).

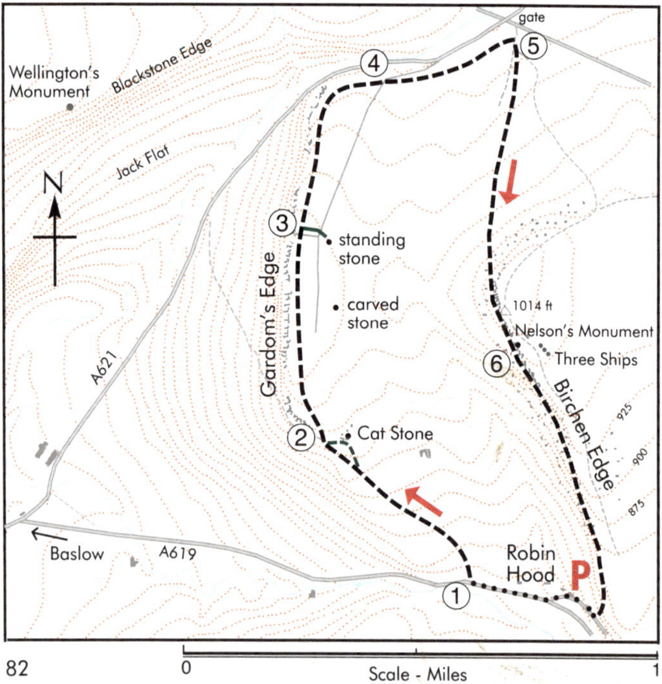

Leave the car park and turn right walking in front of the Robin Hood Inn. Keep on the pavement and in about 120 yards you reach a slanting junction with the main road. Continue along the pavement and in about 180 yards you reach a stile and a footpath sign to the right.

① Go over the stile and walk along the path slanting left uphill. In about 1/3 mile the path levels out. The rocky outcrop ahead and to the right is called the Cat Stone. You can make an optional detour to the stones by taking one of the paths slanting right through bracken. If you look at the face of the rock, above head height, you can see holes that would have secured the ends of timber. This was once a lean-to structure used as a quarryman's hut. If you do go to the Cat Stone return to the main path by taking one of the paths through the bracken. At the main path, bear right to the gap in the wall. If you don't take the detour, just keep on the main path to reach the gap.

② Go through the gap and turn right, walking uphill with the wall to your right. In about 160 yards ignore the gateway to the right, keep on the path by the wall. In another 50 yards go through a gap at the wall corner. Then bear left towards the edge. The three big mounds of stones are called The Three Men. They are supposedly a memorial to three shepherds who died in the snow near here, maybe in the 19th century. They are built on top of an early Bronze Age barrow (burial site).

Continue along the edge. The path winds through silver birch trees. In about 1/3 mile the path crosses a broken wall at a gap, with an old oak tree to the right (see photo 2, on next page). If you look across the valley to the edge opposite you should be able to pick out the stone pillar of Wellington's Monument (just below and to the right of a large rock).

③ Go through the gap and turn right alongside the wall to the gate. Here is an optional diversion to see a standing stone. To visit the standing stone go through the gate, the path passes a tree in 3 yards. Keep straight on for about 8 yards to another tree in line with the first tree and the gate. After this the path splits, one path going straight on and one bearing slightly right. Both of them lead to the standing stone after about 120 yards. The stone is thought to have been erected about 4,000 years ago, during the early Bronze Age. (The British Bronze Age

Walk 16 ~ Gardom's Edge 3 1/4 miles

	Grid references	miles
P	SK2801872137	0.00
①	SK2774972158	0.20
	SK2728872621 Cat Stone	
②	SK2721372602	0.65
③	SK2714873287	1.14
	SK2725473226 standing stone	
	SK2728073040 carved stone	
④	SK2739273780	1.66
⑤	SK2780273944	1.96
⑥	SK2785872908	2.62

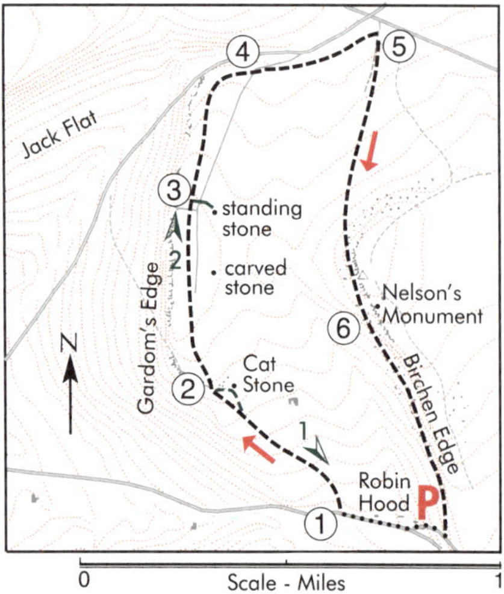

≺ 1 leaving Robin Hood

≺ 2 Gardom's Edge, (near point 3)

standing stone

Nelson's Monument, Birchen Edge

dates are around 2,300 BC - 700BC). The area also contains a piece of Bronze Age rock art. Whilst not part of this diversion you are free to explore. A carved stone is about 200 yards to the south in a grassy clearing (grid reference SK2728073040, easy to find with a GPS, not so easy without). It has carved 'cup and ring' symbols. The stone was discovered in the 1960s, and was buried to preserve it in 1996. The 'stone' you now see is a brilliant resin replica. What do the symbols mean and why is it positioned where it is? From the standing stone return to the gate by the same route. Go through the gate and turn right. (If you don't wish to visit the standing stone, don't go through the gate but turn left). In about 1/2 mile the path bears right to a gate in a wire fence.

(4) Go through the gate and follow the path, the fence to your left. As the fence ends continue on the path which in 1/4 mile descends to a road.

(5) Don't go through the gate to the road, turn sharp right up the path joining from the right. In about 120 yards the path bends left a few feet at a prominent low stone. Before this slight bend ignore a narrow grassy path that goes slightly right and up. Just after the bend ignore the path to the left that goes towards trees. Continue on the wide path heading for the right-hand end of the rocky edge on the skyline. The path gains height as it crosses moorland. It will be a very boggy in places after rain. In 1/2 mile the path reaches the crags of Birchen Edge. You may see people tackling climbs with names such as 'Powder Monkey Parade,' or 'Nelson's Slab.' Continue on the path running beneath the crags and look up. The thin column topped with a ball is Nelson's Monument, hence the climbing route names. It was erected in 1810 to commemorate Nelson's victory at the Battle of Trafalgar in 1805.

(6) When level with the memorial keep to the main path which bears right slightly, going downhill (ignore the path straight ahead going up towards the crags). In 1/2 mile the path passes to the left of a little golf course. As you descend look out for a rock on the right. It has 'ABL' carved on it. Notice the arrow pointing to a bronze stud. This is a bench mark, used by surveyors to locate an accurately measured height. At the end of the path go through the gate, turn right and walk alongside the road (take care, vehicles go too fast along here) back to the car park.

Walk 17 ~ Curbar Edge 2 3/4 miles

Start: Curbar Gap car park, pay-and-display. Free for National Trust members.
GR: SK26217471 **Map:** OS Exp. OL24.
Distance: 3 miles (4.8 km). **Allow:** 1 1/2 hours.
Terrain: Generally well-defined tracks. Keep dogs on a lead and children under close control and always keep a safe distance from the rock edges. Always look where you are walking. Stop when looking at views. A trip, or slip near an edge can be fatal.
Public toilets: None. (Nearest ones are at The Green, Baslow).
Refreshments: At busy times a snack van may be at the car park.
Summary of the Walk: This short route is more or less an out-and-back walk, however the return route follows the edge where possible. There are great views towards the northern Peak District and westwards from the edge. The walk along Curbar Edge is lovely at any time of year, but especially scenic in July or August when the heather is in bloom.
Maximum height: 1115ft (340m). **Ascent:** 147ft (45m).

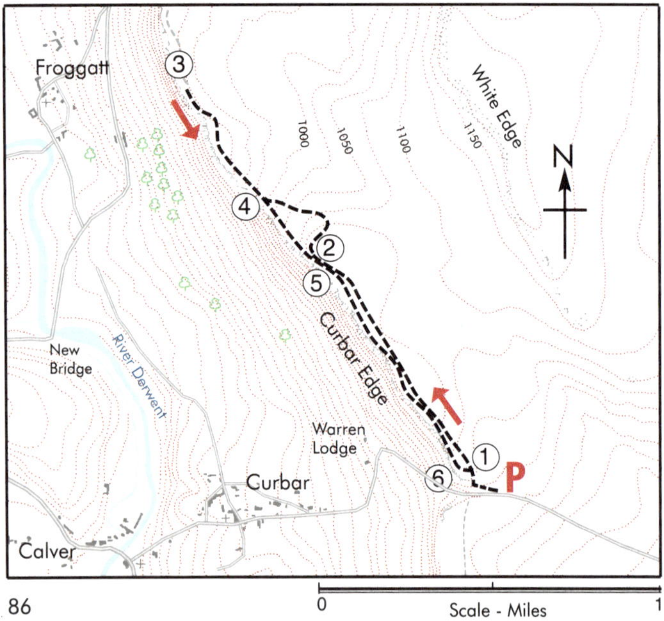

Directions ~ Curbar Edge

From the left corner of the car park (the parking area nearest the road), go up the steps at a sign for 'Curbar Edge.' At the top, turn left.

(1) After about 130 yards, go through the right-hand gate ahead. Keep straight on following a wide track going slightly uphill. In about 1/3 mile the views to the north open out, with Stanage Edge, the northern section of the gritstone edge ahead.

(2) In about 3/4 mile the path splits. A grassy path goes right whilst the path straight on, is a little steeper and rockier. Take either as they both join at the bottom of the hill. If you take the right-hand path, turn right at the junction with the main path in about 220 yards. (Note the post with a yellow arrow, you'll go along here on the way back). Continue along the path, after about 370 yards ignore another signpost and go straight on. Note the distinctively shaped rocks ahead (see photo taken at 'Point 3'). After about 230 yards you'll reach these rocks. The views all around are excellent. To the left of the edge (the northerly direction) you'll see Win Hill, with the bluish strip of land on the horizon being Kinder Scout. The distant edge to the right of these is Bamford Edge, which overlooks Ladybower Reservoir. The flat-topped hill further to the right in the distance is Higger Tor.

(3) From the rocks turn round and walk with the edge to your right. Rather than keeping on the main wide path on the return route, you may prefer to follow the grassy paths running alongside the edge. It makes a change and the views are better. In about 230 yards ignore the signpost to the right. In a further 370 yards you reach the signpost at the bottom of the hill, noted earlier.

(4) Go straight on here, along a narrow path. In about 50 yards ignore a post pointing to a path downhill. Keep to the edge path, bearing left slightly and going uphill. In about 250 yards look out for half a millstone lying alongside the path. Whether you notice the stone or not, ignore the path to the left, just after the remnant of an old wall, and continue straight on up a grassy path. Follow the well defined path as it bears left in front of rocks. (Don't be tempted to go straight on along grass between rock walls). It then bends right to join the main wide path.

(5) Keep to the narrower paths along the edge, giving views rather than

Walk 17 ~ Curbar Edge 3 miles

	Grid references	miles
P	SK2621474712	0.00
①	SK2612774766	0.08
②	SK2542775698	0.83
③	SK2493176321	1.14
④	SK2521975908	1.41
⑤	SK2544175645	1.77
⑥	SK2604874777	2.77

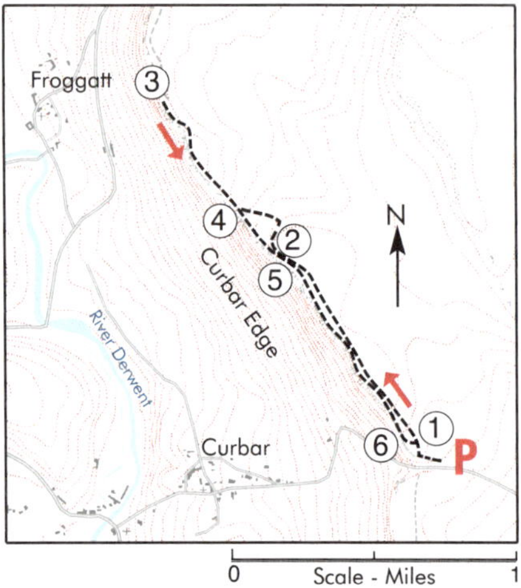

rocks at 'Point 3'

millstone on Curbar Edge

Curbar Edge, with Baslow Edge behind

following the wide path (of course use that if you wish). Along the edge look out for more remnants of the once thriving millstone industry. The stones were cut from the solid rock and gradually worked into a perfect round shape with a hole in the middle for a spindle. You should see stones that have only been partly worked and left in an unfinished state. They were finished 'on site' and then transported all over to mills for grinding cereal grain. The gritstone millstones were mainly used to grind barley which was then used for animal feed. They weren't suitable for grinding wheat for human consumption as they contaminated the grain with stone dust and chips. After the end of the Napoleonic Wars in 1815 imports of cheaper French burrstones resumed. These were not cut from a single piece of rock but constructed of segments of quartz, cemented with plaster and bound on the outer edge with an iron band. They came from the Marne Valley in northern France. The cleaner grinding and longer lasting stones were suitable for grinding grains into flour for human consumption and more or less ended the Derbyshire industry at a stroke. Hence the reason why you see abandoned gritstone millstones, even though some of them are in a finished state. Spare a thought for the skilful stone masons who created these beautiful stones from the rough rock, working out here in all weathers throughout the year. Their lives would be so different from ours and yet they somehow connect with us through their enduring work.

Most modern bulk produced flour is now made from grains ground with rollers rather than stones, but stone-ground flour is still made by specialist millers. The traditional Derbyshire millstone was chosen as the symbol of the Peak District National Park.

The rock that forms the Derbyshire edges is gritstone. However to be geologically correct it is classed as a sandstone. The gritty, rough texture is due to it having pebbles embedded in it. It also sometimes contains quartz, a hard white crystalline mineral that glints in the sun.

⑥ After about 3/4 mile of walking along the edge, the path bends left to rejoin the main, wide path at the prominent white gate. Go through the gate and continue straight on, ignoring the path bearing right. Retrace your outward steps to the car park.

Walk 18 ~ Baslow Edge 1 3/4 miles

Start: Curbar Gap car park. Pay-and-display. Free for National Trust members.
GR: SK26217471. **Map:** OS Exp. OL24.
Distance: 1 3/4 miles (2.8 km). **Allow:** 1 hour.
Terrain: Sandy track. Grassy paths. Sometimes a little rocky underfoot.
Public toilets: None.
Refreshments: Occasionally there is a refreshment van at the car park.
Summary of the Walk: A short, easy, more or less level walk sampling one of Derbyshire's renowned gritstone edges, Baslow Edge. The walk begins by taking the wide path across moorland, passing the large boulder known as the Eagle Stone. At the end of the path there are great views along the valley, towards Chatsworth Park. Just to the left is a stone cross, Wellington's Monument. The return section follows a winding path along Baslow Edge with views along the edge and across the hills to the west.
Maximum height: 1049ft (320m). **Ascent:** 147ft (45m).

	Grid references	miles
P	SK2621474712	0.00
①	SK2606774619	0.11
	SK2624973835 Eagle Stone	0.63
②	SK2629373690	0.74
	SK2642073686 Wellington's Mon.	0.82
③	SK2599874568	1.63

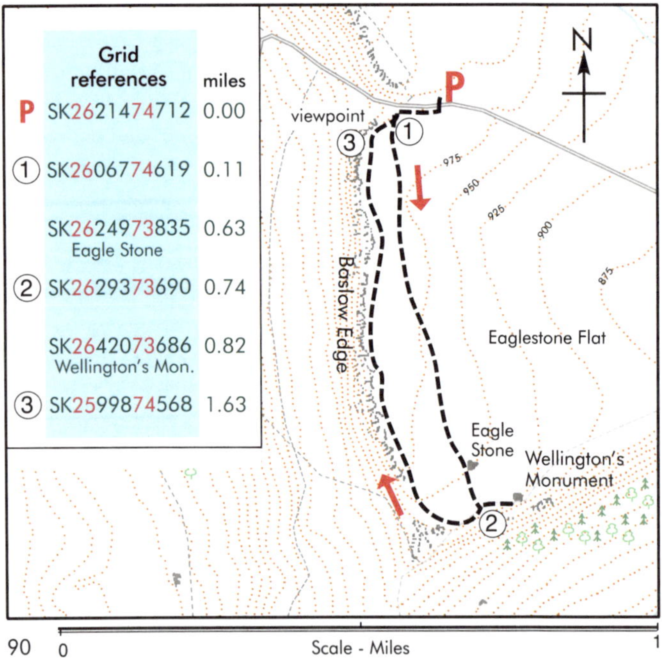

Leave the car park by the right-hand roadside corner (right, if you are facing the entrance) along a path signed 'Wheelchair access Baslow Edge.' Cross the road and follow the wide path opposite. Ignore the first gate (no access) and in 30 yards you reach the footpath access gate. Go through the gate and follow the wide path.

① In about 20 yards ignore the narrower path to the right. Keep on the wide path. The path leads across the Eaglestone Flat, an area of moorland and in 1/2 mile you reach a distinctive large boulder, called the Eagle Stone. It is said that in 'days gone by' young men from nearby Baslow had to climb the stone, to prove themselves worthy of marriage. It is a lot more difficult than it looks! The rock is sandstone, however the stone which forms this rock and all the 'edges' is known as gritstone. It is roughly textured and often has pebbles embedded in it. It also con tains a lot of quartz, a white crystalline mineral that glints in the sun.

Continue past the Eagle Stone, having conquered it or not. In 180 yards you come to a junction with another path at a broad edge. The gritstone edge across the broad valley to the left is Gardom's Edge and straight ahead the view along the valley includes Chatsworth Park.

② Turn left and make a short detour to see a chunky stone-built cross, Wellington's Monument. This was constructed in 1866 to commemorate the Duke of Wellington's victory at Waterloo in 1815. It was paid for by a local doctor, Dr. Wrench. He was an ex-army man and wanted a military memorial to compliment Nelson's Monument, on nearby Birchen Edge. Retrace your steps, ignoring the path to your right (the one you were on) and the wide track slanting downhill. Walk straight on, going up along a narrow path. This meanders along Baslow Edge, its weather-worn rocks providing the foreground to beautiful views across and along the valley. After about 1/2 mile the path is indistinct as it crosses a grassy area. Keep straight on going slightly uphill. In about 200 yards you pass a viewpoint, a steel etched plaque detailing the panorama.

③ From the viewpoint the route continues along the surfaced path. Follow this to the junction with the wide path and turn left. In a few yards go through the small gate on the right hand side and retrace steps back to the car park.

Walk 19 ~ Eyam and Riley Graves 3 1/2 miles

Start: Free car park, Hawkhill Road, Eyam. Note - closes 5.00pm Oct-March. 8.00pm April-Sep. Or the pay-and-display car park just before the free car park, which is open all the time.
GR: SK21667669. **Map:** OS Exp. OL24.
Distance: 3 1/2 miles (4.8 km). **Allow:** 2 hours.
Terrain: Lanes in Eyam and Stoney Middleton. Field paths and a stony lane. The fairly steep lane leading down into Stoney Middleton (between points 5 and 6) is sometimes used by off-road motor cyclists, usually on Sundays. It can get muddy. The path up to the Boundary Stone is steep.
Public toilets: Hawkhill Road pay-and-display car park, Eyam.
Refreshments: Cafés and pub in Eyam.
Summary of the Walk: Eyam is also known as 'The Plague Village,' because of the outbreak of the disease in 1665/6. This walk takes you to most of the main features associated with that period - the 'plague cottages', Cucklet Church, the Boundary Stone and Riley Graves. Leaving Eyam the route gains height giving views towards the gritstone edges, passing Riley Graves before descending into Stoney Middleton. From there a fairly steep hill leads to the Boundary Stone and back into Eyam. There is an optional 1/2 mile diversion to see Eyam Delf and Cucklet Church.
Maximum height: 984ft (300m). **Ascent:** 459ft (140m).

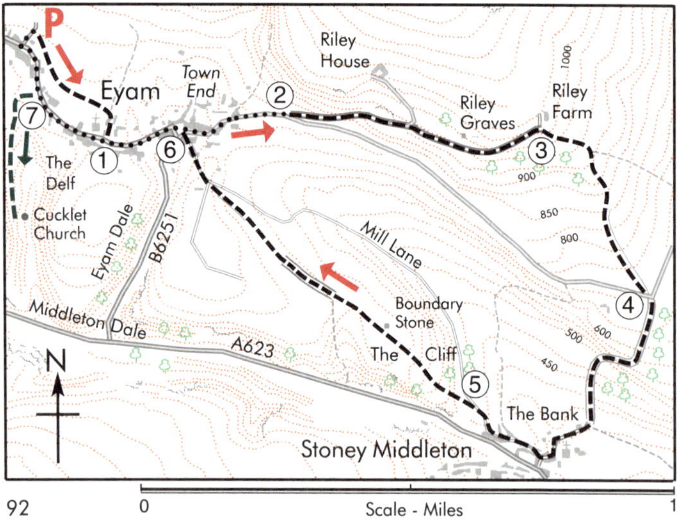

A note about the car park. Just past the Hawkhill Road pay-and-display car park, there is a free car park (donations welcome). If you think you'll finish your walk after the car park closes, use the pay-and-display car park. Then turn left at its exit, walk down the road to the junction, turn left and pick up the instructions at the church - (point 1).

From the free car park walk to the top right-hand corner (diagonally opposite the entrance) Follow the gravel path to the side of the gate Pass a childrens' play area to your right, keep straight on ignoring the gate to the right. Go through the gate ahead, and in 180 yards turn right at a gate, through the churchyard to the road. It's worth looking around and going in the church to see the register of plague deaths. The Eyam Plague of 1665/66 began when the tailor had delivery of a case of cloth. The cloth was infested with rat fleas, which carried the disease, but at the time it wasn't known how the disease was spread. The tailor's assistant, George Viccars was the first victim, dying on 7th September 1665. It then spread quickly through the village claiming the lives of whole families. In the winter the disease abated, but with warmer weather in the late spring and summer it flared up again. The villagers were persuaded by the vicar, William Mompesson to quarantine themselves to prevent the disease spreading to surrounding villages and towns. About 270 people died, all within the Eyam boundary.

① Go through the gap and turn left along the road, (Church Street) after passing a school it descends into an open area 'The Square.' Keep straight on, passing a café to your left, with another opposite. In 150 yards ignore a lane to the left (Riley Back Lane). Continue for 100 yards.

② Turn left up the lane 'Riley Lane.' The tarmac lane gains height giving good views. In 1/4 mile keep straight on, ignoring the turn for Riley House Farm. In about 200 yards you'll reach Riley Graves, go over the stile to the walled enclosure. A poignant memorial of the plague. It contains gravestones of the Hancock family. The mother, Elizabeth, buried her husband, two sons and four daughters, all within eight days.

③ In another 200 yards bear right, ignoring the private lane ahead. The path goes through woodland and then winds down to a path junction. Turn right here, downhill. In just under 1/4 mile you reach a road.

Walk 19 ~ Eyam and Riley Graves 3 1/2 miles

	Grid references	miles
P	SK2165976699	0.00
①	SK2179576380	0.27
②	SK2228576464	0.60
③	SK2302776378	1.09
④	SK2344275952	1.51
⑤	SK2292375588	2.14
⑥	SK2204376390	2.91
⑦	SK2159876512	3.23

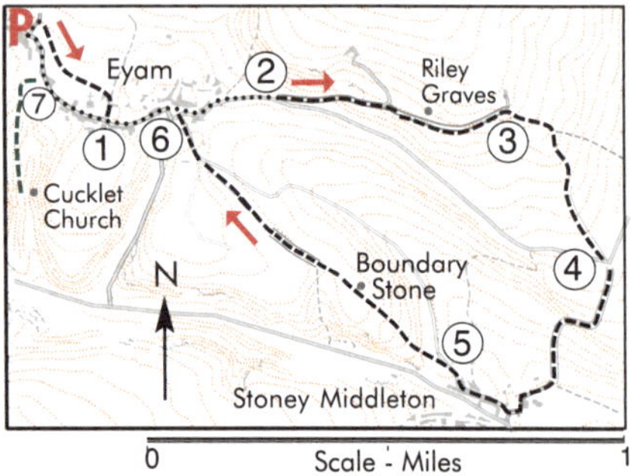

Riley Graves

Boundary Stone

Plague Cottages, Eyam

(4) Cross over (it's a blind corner and safer to walk to the right first to give a better view). At the corner opposite (before reaching a footpath sign) is a narrow unsurfaced lane going downhill. Turn sharp right here. At the bottom it bends right, joining a road into Stoney Middleton. You pass the 'Roman Baths,' not Roman but dating to the nineteenth century. Ignore the road to the left and go straight on. The road then bends left, passing a church and then bends right going uphill. At the road junction, turn right going uphill. In about 100 yards bear right uphill to a sign 'The Fold'. Then turn left (footpath sign 'Eyam') up a lane called 'Cliff Bottom.' In 140 yards you pass an 'unsuitable for motors' sign.

(5) In 20 yards a footpath sign points left, go through the gate and walk up the steep grassy hill. As you near the top, in about 1/4 mile head for the clump of tall trees. You'll then see a squat stone, this is the Boundary Stone. During the plague coins were left in vinegar filled holes, in return for supplies; preventing contact with 'outsiders.' Go straight on, the path leading to a walled lane. This ends and a track crosses fields to a gap at a gate next to a house. In about 90 yards you join a road. Go straight on. In about 100 yards ignore a road to the left, keep straight on pass ing the Lydgate Graves to your left. At the bottom is a road junction.

(6) Cross over and turn left walking back up Church Street. After passing the church, on the right is a row of 'plague cottages.' Further on is Eyam Hall. Opposite is the village green, an information barn and the stocks. 100 yards beyond on the left is New Close, opposite the craft centre.

(7) For a 1/4 mile (each way) detour to Cucklet Church turn left along New Close. In 80 yards turn left along Dunlow Lane. In 100 yards, where the road bends right, go straight on, signed 'Eyam Delf and Cucklet Church.' Follow the track and in 150 yards turn left through a gate, at a sign 'Cucklet Church.' The path leads to an open area with a limestone arch. In the plague, so that villagers could worship without being confined in church, William Mompesson held services here. The villagers on the grass, whilst he used the top of the arch as a pulpit. Return the same way to the main road. Turn left and in 300 yards turn right up Hawkhill Road back to the car park. **If you don't take the diversion**, just substitute 'go straight on' for the first two words of the previous sentence.

Walk 20 ~ Bretton Clough 3 1/2 miles

Start: Lay-by, at the west end of Sir William Hill Road. **GR:** SK21027775. **Map:** OS Exp. OL24.
Distance: 3 1/2 miles (5.6 km). **Allow:** 2 hours.
Terrain: Stony tracks, grassy paths, one short boggy section. Just one fairly steep uphill. Several step-stiles.
Public toilets: None.
Refreshments: None. (Inn at Bretton nearby).
Summary of the Walk: A walk around Bretton Clough, a secluded and beautiful valley. There are far reaching views towards the northern Peak hills of Mam Tor and Kinder Scout and eastwards to the gritstone edges. The route gradually descends along a grassy path into Bretton Clough, a short detour brings you to Stoke Ford, a meeting place of two streams. From here the route follows the narrow valley, before taking an old farm track winding up and back onto open land, giving more great views.
Maximum height: 1247ft (380m). **Ascent:** 590ft (180m).

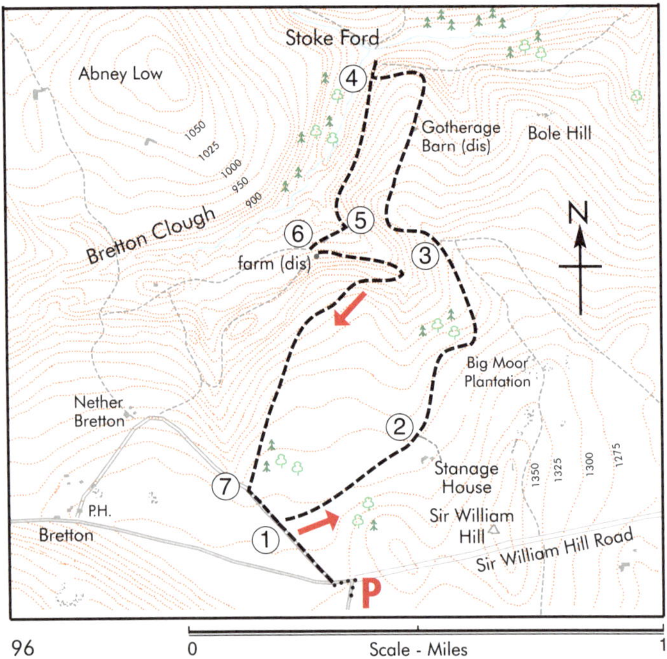

From the parking area walk down to the road corner, ignore the track leaving to the right and continue along the road for about 50 yards. Turn right along the stony track signed 'Byway open to all traffic.'

(1) In 1/4 mile turn right over a stile (or through a gate), signed 'Stoke Ford.' The wide path runs along a wall. In 1/3 mile the wide track bends right.

(2) Keep straight on here, there is a white arrow on a stone. A grassy path runs to the right of a wall enclosing woodland. In about 150 yards go over the stone step-stile and keep straight on, the wall still to your left. In about 300 yards go over another step-stile and bear left, the wall still to your left. The path descends gently, with moorland to your right. When you clear the trees there are lovely views across the valley. The hills in the middle distance are neatly divided into walled fields, making sheltered pasture for sheep. They would have once been open moorland, like the heather-covered land to your right. In the far distance you should be able to make out the distinctive triangular shape of Mam Tor's south face. The greenish-grey strip of hills to its right is the southern edge of Kinder Scout. In about 200 yards a gate blocks the path ahead.

(3) Go over the stile in the wall just before the gate and continue on the wide path as it descends into the valley. In a field to the right you may see a ruined building. This is Gotherage Barn, near here was Gotherage Farm which was the scene of a murder in 1785. A local man known as Blinker Bland and some other men came to the farm at night. They mistakenly thought money was hidden there. When the farmer recognised him, Blinker hit him over the head with a milking stool, killing him. The farmer's wife raised the alarm at a farm in Bretton and it is thought that the men were caught to face justice. In about 300 yards there is another step stile. The view to the right soon opens up along the valley eastwards. The flat-topped ramparts of Higger Tor on the horizon and Stanage Edge to its left. The path begins to descend more steeply, then bends to the left going through a wooded area. It then bends to the right before meeting a path junction.

(4) For an 80 yard diversion to Stoke Ford, turn right, walking down to the lovely meeting place of two streams, an ideal rest spot. Then retrace steps back to this junction and walk straight on. Alternatively turn left

Walk 20 ~ Bretton Clough 3 1/2 miles

	Grid references	miles
P	SK2102077750	0.00
①	SK2074577926	0.25
②	SK2120378191	0.59
③	SK2126278888	1.12
④	SK2109379470	1.68
⑤	SK2096678899	2.14
⑥	SK2085778821	2.28
⑦	SK2061678053	3.12

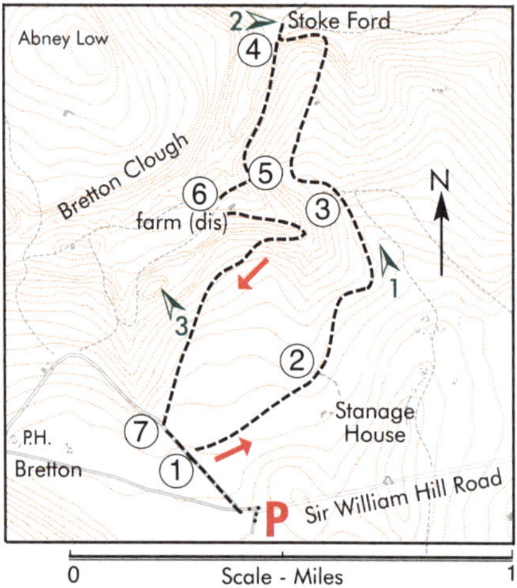

1 above Bretton Clough

2 at Stoke Ford

3 looking north across Bretton Clough to Abney

here following the path along the slopes of the clough. The narrow path passes through woods, going through a gate and in another 200 yards reaches another gate. A boggy pond is ahead, a low cliff to the left.

5 Turn right, initially with a fence to your right, the grassy path climbs fairly steeply. In about 100 yards it passes beneath a ruined building, above and to the left of you. When about level with building you cross a fragmentary broken wall. In another 15 yards you cross a second broken wall and after about 50 yards you reach a third and more intact broken wall. (If you get confused - after this final wall is an open field ahead).

6 Turn sharp left just after the wall, walking up and along the old farm track and in about 100 yards you'll pass to the right of the ruin, previously noted. This used to be a farm, one of two in the area that have long since been abandoned. The secluded valley was used as a safe haven by the people of Eyam in 1745 who kept their livestock here with the approach of about 6,000 Highlanders led by Prince Charles Edward Louis John Casmir Sylvester Severino Maria Stuart. Also known as Bonnie Prince Charlie or The Young Pretender, he was on his way to attack London. He made it as far as Swarkestone Bridge, just south of Derby. He and his army retreated back to Scotland, then lost to the English at the Battle of Culloden in April 1746. He escaped from the Isle of Skye, disguised as Flora MacDonald's maid and eventually reached France. In 30 yards there is another ruined building to your right. Continue along the track as it goes further up and along the steep-sided valley. After about 300 yards the track bends to the right, passing beneath power cables. (It may be a little boggy around here). It then climbs quite steeply. In about 80 yards go through a gate and then another gate in a further 100 yards. Ignore the path bearing right, continue straight on. The track runs alongside a broken wall gaining height gradually. There are now good views to the right, over the clough. The few scattered farms that you can see make up the hamlet of Abney. The distant horizon is again the high ground of Kinder Scout.

7 In 1/3 mile ignore a path veering right, keep straight on, then go through a small gate and in 180 yards you reach a junction with the stony lane. Turn left, retracing outward steps for 1/4 mile to the finish.

Walk 21 ~ Longshaw Estate 2 3/4 miles

Start: Woodcroft car park, Longshaw Estate. Pay-and-display. Free for National Trust members.
GR: SK26658006. **Map:** OS Exp. OL24.
Distance: 2 3/4 miles (4.4 km). **Allow:** 1 1/2 hours.
Terrain: Surfaced tracks, grassy paths, can be muddy. Only one gentle uphill. No stiles.
Public toilets: At the Visitor's Centre.
Refreshments: Café at the Visitor's Centre.
Summary of the Walk: A pleasant short walk in the beautiful Longshaw Estate, owned by the National Trust. There are expansive views to the north and west over the Dark Peak hills and valleys. The route follows the main wide track through the estate, before descending to an area of beautiful Scots pines. A grassy path leads through the estate passing a lovely pond and following a surfaced path back to the visitor's centre and car park.
Maximum height: 1135ft (346m). **Ascent:** 180ft (55m).

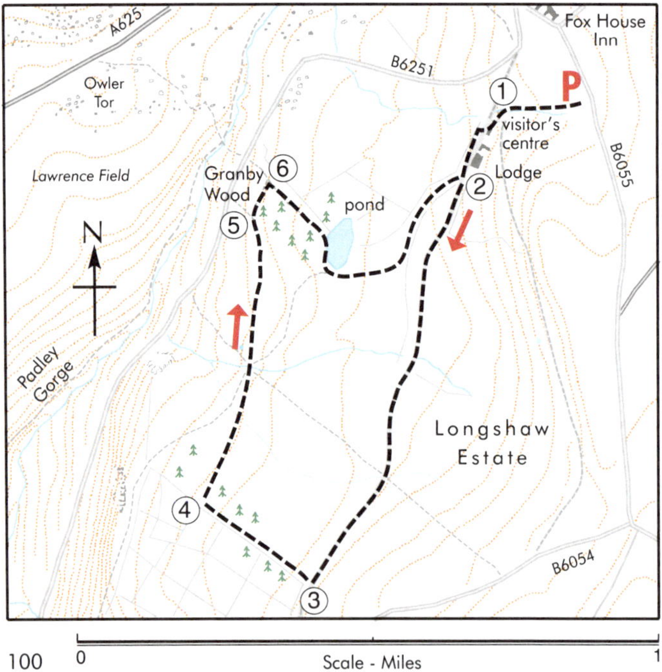

Follow the wide path down from the car park, signed 'Visitor Centre.'

(1) Go over the bridge and in about 40 yards turn right, signed 'Visitor Centre and Estate Walks.' In 20 yards ignore the path to the left signed 'Visitor Centre' and continue straight on. In about 50 yards you reach a junction with the estate road. Cross over and follow a path signed 'footpath' descending steps by a fence. The large field ahead is Longshaw Meadow, where the Longshaw Sheep Dog Trials are held every year on the first weekend in September. The first one took place in 1898 and it is thought they are the longest running trials in the country. If you look to your right you'll see two distinctive flat-topped hills. The nearer and lower one is Carl Wark, thought to have been used as a fort during the Iron Age (around 800BC - 100AD). The summit has an earth rampart and a stone wall, which may have formed part of a defensive structure.

Behind you, set back to the right of the visitor's centre is Longshaw Lodge. The Estate was owned by the Duke of Rutland and then covered a much larger area. The Lodge was built in the late 1820s by the 5th Duke of Rutland (John Manners 1778-1857) as a shooting lodge. It was referred to dismissively as only a 'shooting box.' It is now privately occupied and not open to the public. Most of the wide paths or 'drives' running through the estate were made by successive Dukes of Rutland to provide easy access to their grouse shooting moors. Without their ownership a lot of the moorland and diversity of landscape may have been lost to agriculture. In 1927 the Estate was sold off in lots. About 3,000 acres were bought by Sheffield Council. They intended to construct a reservoir as a supply for the city. Thankfully this didn't happen, due mainly to public opposition. Money was raised by the public and in 1931, part of their land was handed to the National Trust. This now forms the Longshaw Estate as it is today, about 750 acres compared to the original size of about 11,000 acres. The council retained the rest of their land and still own it for the public' benefit. (The moorland area containing Carl Wark and Higger Tor is owned by them).

(2) Continue along the path alongside a fence, the meadow to your right. Go through the gate, passing a millstone, ignore the path to the right and in few yards go through another gate. Continue straight on along

Walk 21 ~ Longshaw Estate

2 1/2 miles

	Grid references	miles
P	SK2665080060	0.00
1	SK2650679997	0.11
2	SK2636479856	0.27
3	SK2595078801	1.00
4	SK2564879005	1.29
5	SK2580879748	1.80
6	SK2584979847	1.88

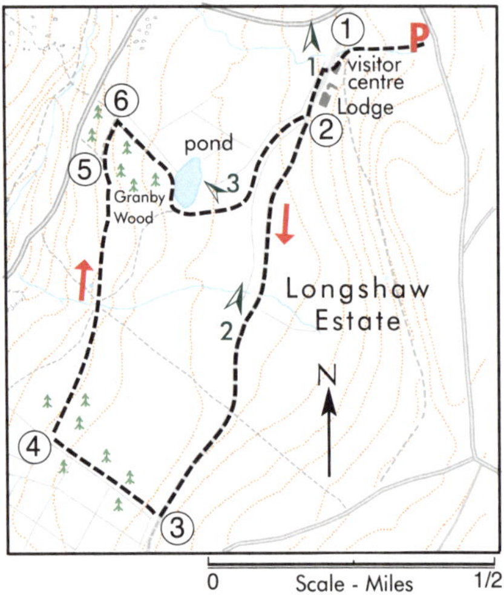

≺ 1 Carl Wark and Higger Tor, from Longshaw Meadow

≺ 2 Longshaw Estate

≺ 3 Longshaw Pond

the wide track, which gives good views towards the west. You will see the distinctive peak of Mam Tor on the skyline. The Estate contains many types of landscape, from open moorland, rough grass, woodland and wet areas. This provides a great diversity of habitats that encourages birds, plants and animals. In 1/3 mile you pass between two substantial stone gateposts. In 300 yards keep straight on at a path crossroads, signed 'Grouse Inn.' In 1/4 mile a gate crosses the track.

③ Turn right just before the gate, going through a small gate and follow a path downhill, between a wall on the left and woods to the right. You may see large dome-shaped structures on the right-hand side. These are nests made by the hairy northern wood ant. Please don't touch. The path ends after about 370 yards at a gate. Keep straight on for about 40 yards, with a wall to your left, until you reach two gates in the wall.

④ Turn right when level with the first gate, following a grassy path through the scattered scots pines. After 1/4 mile the path crosses a stream at a path crossroads. Keep straight on, the path gaining height and in about 1/4 mile you reach a gate.

⑤ Go through the gate into woodland. This is Granby Wood, named after the Duke's son, The Marquess of Granby (The 5th Duke had four sons, two of whom died in infancy, both called John). A Marquess is heir to a Dukedom, in which case it is a courtesy title. However it can also be a rank of nobility in its own right, with the holder being part of a Marquessate, rather than a Dukedom. Dukes can also use the term Marquess as a subsidiary title, which just adds to the confusion.

⑥ In about 150 yards turn right at a path junction, in 70 yards go through a gate and straight on to a beautifully situated pond. This is Longshaw Pond. It isn't natural but was probably dug in about 1830, around about the time that the Lodge was built. It used to have a boathouse and pier. Maybe the Duke's guests who didn't wish to go shooting would while away a few pleasant hours here. Keep on the path going through two more gates. About 160 yards past the second gate, you'll pass a mill-stone at a path junction. Turn left here going through a gate, you're now on the same path that you set out on. Retrace steps to the car park or of course you may wish to call in at the Visitor Centre en-route.

16	Martin & Shirley 29.1.17

Useful Addresses

Peak District National Park Authority
Aldern House
Baslow Road
Bakewell DE45 1AE
Tel: 01629 816200
web: www.peakdistrict.org
email: customer.service@peakdistrict.gov.uk

Youth Hostels Association (YHA)
Trevelyan House
Dimple Road
Matlock
Derbyshire DE4 3YH
Tel: 01629 592600
web: www.yha.org.uk

Ramblers' Association
2nd Floor
Camelford House
87-90 Albert Embankment
London SE1 7TW
Tel 020 7339 8500
web: www.ramblers.org

Tourist Information Centre
Old Market Hall
Bridge Street
Bakewell DE45 1DS
Tel: 01629 813227
Email: bakewell@peakdistrict-npa.gov.uk

Reporting path problems:
Derbyshire County Council (Highways Authority)
County Hall
Matlock
DE4 3AG
Tel 0845 6058058 or 01629 736200
website: www.derbyshire.gov.uk
email: contact.centre@derbyshire.gov.uk

Bibliography

Below is a list of Peak District and Derbyshire related books that may be of interest. The date given is the year of first publication. Many are out of print, but you should be able to find copies at - www.abebooks.com or www.amazon.co.uk. (also at real bookshops).

The Best of the Sheffield Clarion Ramblers' Handbook - Ward's Piece, Edited by David Sissons. Halsgrove 2002.

Byways, Boots and Blisters, Bill Laws. Sutton Publishing 2008.

Derbyshire in the Civil War, Brian Stone. Scarthin Books 1992.

First and Last, Roland Smith. Peak Park Joint Planning Board 1978.

Freedom to Roam, Howard Hill. Moorland 1980.

Geology Explained in the Peak District, FW Cope. Scarthin Books 1988.

The Guide Stoops of the Dark Peak, H Smith. H Smith 1999.

Hanged for a Sheep - Crime in bygone Derbyshire, EG Power. Scarthin Books 1988.

Highways and Byways in Derbyshire, JB Frith. MacMillan & Co. 1905.

High Peak, Eric Byne and Geoffrey Sutton. Secker & Warburg 1966.

Kinder Scout, Edited by Roly Smith. Various publishers 2002.

Lead Mining in the Peak District, Peak District Mines Historical Society. Peak Park Joint Planning Board 1968.

Moors, Crags and Caves of the High Peak, EA Baker. Heywood 1903 (reprinted by Halsgrove, 2002.)

Mountain Rescue - History and Development in the Peak District, Ian Hurst, Roger Bennet. Tempus Publishing 2007.

Odd Corners in Derbyshire, William Palmer. Skeffington & Son 1938.

The Peak and Pennines, WA Poucher. Constable 1966.

The Peak District Café Guide, A McCloy, Johnson Publishing 2003.

The Peak District Pub Guide, A McCloy, Johnson Publishing 2002.

Peakland Lead Mines and Miners, HM Parker. Moorland 1979.

Peakland Pubs - A Pint-Sized History, Andrew McCloy. Halsgrove 2005.

Peak District Place Names, Martin Spray. John N Merrill 1989.

Round About Chatsworth, The Dowager Duchess of Devonshire. Frances Lincoln 2005.

Scenic Walks in the Peak District, Johnson Publishing 2010.

It Could Be a Little Gold Mine - Tales of a Derbyshire Innkeeper, David Allingham. Illustrations by Bill Tidy. Johnson Publishing 2005.

Index (walks section only)

Index (walks section only)

Index (walks section only)